Testimonies

Of

Ex-Muslims

Compiled by

Commander Michael H. Imhof,
U.S. Navy (ret.)

Evangel Press
Nappanee, IN

Printed by **Evangel Press**
2000 Evangel Way
Nappanee, IN 46550
www.evangelpress.com

Printed in the United States of America

Imhof, Michael H.
        Testimonies of Ex-Muslims / by Michael H. Imhof
        p. cm.
        ISBN **1-933858-01-X**
1.   2.   I.

Library of Congress Control Number 2006922311

"I make a decree,
that in every dominion of my kingdom
men tremble and fear before the God of Daniel:
for he is the living God, and steadfast for ever,
and his kingdom that which shall not be destroyed,
and his dominion shall be even unto the end."
Daniel 6:26

"Jesus saith unto him,
I am the way, the truth, and the life:
no man cometh unto the Father,
but by me."
John 14:6

CONTENTS

FOREWORD

I was living in Afghanistan when the idea came to me about putting together a small book of testimonies from ex-Muslims. Many people have been so misled by the religion of Islam. In many cases, Muslims are very sincere in their beliefs, but that does not make their beliefs correct. Truth, in reality, is more important than sincerity.

Although I've never been a Muslim, a believer of Islam, I've talked to numerous Muslims over time, and have studied this religion to some extent. My findings have been conclusive; it is a false religion. Based on my review and comparison of the Bible and the Koran, I know unequivocally that Jehovah is not Allah. These books could not have been written or ordained by the same god. There are substantive differences between the Christian and Islamic religions.

The testimonies of the ex-Muslims in this book reveal how they found the truth and escaped the bondage of Islam. Let me say it's not an easy decision to leave Islam, because the Koran calls for death to those who leave this religion. Parents will disown their own children for leaving Islam. Thus, there's a big price to pay when a Muslim makes a decision for Christianity. Severe persecution is common for ex-Muslims who renounce the teachings of the Koran. Make no mistake; it takes courage and strong convictions to make life-changing decisions of this nature.

Some names have been replaced with pseudo names in some of these testimonies for their own personal protection. The content and style of these chapters have been presented the way the people have presented their testimonies. I have obtained permission to use each testimony in this book. They have given me permission because they want to exalt Jesus Christ in their lives, and in the lives of others. To God be all glory.

Michael H. Imhof
Commander, U. S. Navy, (ret.)

INTRODUCTION

Many people in the world believe that Muslims and Christians serve the same God under different names, but that's not so. Most assuredly, Allah of the Koran is not Jehovah of the Bible. They are not the same deities.

I've lived in Afghanistan, Egypt, Jordan and Israel. I've conducted liaison with the Palestinian Liberation Organization and Israeli Defense Forces. I've formed some pretty strong opinions on the differences between Muslims, Jews and Christians. I will now share a few thoughts on Islam, as objective as I can be.

Muhammad, the prophet of Islam, was born in 570 A.D. in Mecca. Muhammad's father died before he was born, and his mother died when he was still young. According to the *Cyclopedia of Biblical, Theological, and Ecclesiastical Literature,* Muhammad's mother often claimed she was visited by spirits and that she had visions and religious experiences, too. Some scholars today believe she was actually involved in occult practices and that this basic orientation was inherited by her son.[1]

According to tradition Muhammad would often fall down on the ground, his body would begin to jerk, his eyes would roll backwards, and he would perspire profusely when he was about to receive a divine revelation from Allah. *The Shorter Encyclopedia of Islam* points out that the Hadith, another collection of Islamic sacred writings, describes "the half-abnormal ecstatic condition with which he was overcome." [2] Based on this type of bodily action during his trances, some scholars believe he was actually having epileptic seizures.

It's interesting to note, that on one occasion, according to scholar Alfred Guillaume, Muhammad claimed that a heavenly being had split open his stomach, stirred his insides around, and then sewed him back up.[3]

The Koran in Sura 4:3 forbids the taking of more than four wives. Muslim scholar Ali Dashti indicates Muhammad had at least 16 wives, along with slaves and concubines, according to author and scholar Robert Morey. Aesha, one of his wives, was only eight or nine years old when he consummated the marriage.[4] This is interesting since the Koran was supposed to have been revealed to man through Muhammad.

Western countries heard the term "Holy Jihad" from Saddam Hussein during the Gulf War. People in the West, in most cases, do not understand how that term came into being as part of the Islamic religion. Basically, Muhammad tried to get people to accept his prophet-hood and follow his teachings through persuasion, but that didn't work out too well. People weren't as receptive as he desired. He then turned to force and violence to subdue the people into following his teachings. To participate in Jihad was to conduct religious fighting on behalf of Allah's cause. The Hadith, a record of Muhammad's words and deeds according to wives, relatives, and close companions, even reveals that Muhammad wanted his religion spread primarily by the sword.

Muhammad demanded that Muslims force Jews, Christians and pagans to embrace Islam or submit to violent consequences if they didn't. People regularly see this principle of Jihad at work today in Islamic countries. Look at the countries of Nigeria and Sudan: hundreds of thousands of Christians and pagans have been brutally slaughtered or enslaved in the name of Jihad because they would not convert to Islam.

Western nations will never understand why Muslims think and act the way they do until they acknowledge that Islam is an Arabian cultural religion. Seventh-century Arabia appears whenever fundamentalism Islam is dominant. You see, Muhammad took all the secular and sacred customs of the culture around him and incorporated them into Islam. All aspects of life are dictated by Islam; it's a way of life. Look at Iran under the influence of Islamic clergy, as a case in point.

Notice how Islamic countries do not typically have democracies. Muhammad took the political laws of seventh-century Arabian tribes and made them into the laws of Allah. The one in charge of the tribe or group had absolute authority over those under him. There was no concept of personal rights in seventh-century Arabia. This is why today you still see many Arab nations ruled by despots or tyrants.

Many will notice a crescent moon symbol on some Middle Eastern flags and mosques. In reality, the crescent moon was a pagan symbol of moon-god worship in Arabian culture and elsewhere throughout the Middle East. The moon god was known as "Allah" by many in pre-Islamic Arabia. According to Middle East scholar E.M. Wherry, pre-Islamic Allah-worship and the worship of Ba-al, were both astral religions in that they involved the worship of the sun, the moon, and the stars.[5] The historical background of the Arabian "Allah" does not greatly support him as being the same God of the biblical patriarchs, Jews, and Christians.

As one earnestly studies the life and teachings of Muhammad one can only come to the conclusion that this religion was not inspired by God. A religion greatly influenced by paganism, it was founded in violence and spread through violence. The Koran is full of inconsistencies and historical errors. The Hadith goes on to reveal bizarre and outlandish assertions by Muhammad that befuddle common sense and intelligent reasoning. A religion that's exceptionally oppressive to women, it has unfortunately misled billions.

So much can be said on Islam. I've only provided a few comments to convey some basic insight on Allah, Muhammad, the Koran and the Hadith. Now please allow these dear ex-Muslims the opportunity to share with you why they decided to leave this oppressive religion and accept the gospel of Jesus Christ and His wonderful love into their lives.

CHAPTER 1

Ali's Story

I was born in eastern Kurdistan (Iran). My parents were nominal Muslims and I never really gave much thought to religion. At a very young age, I was sent to an Islamic school to learn the Qur'an but I dropped out after a few months and never went back. All of the washing and different times for prayers never made sense to me. Whenever there was talk about religion, I would just become sick in the stomach. I hated religion. I have always thought that it was something that enslaved people and that religious people were dumb.

Because of my dad's political activity and his troubles with the Iranian police, we had to leave our homeland. After a few years we settled in the West. Life became a hell. Discrimination was everywhere. Not knowing what to do, I started hanging out with the wrong people. Without thinking twice, I started experimenting with drugs even though it was hard for me to get my hands on them. My friends and I would drink every Saturday night and watch pornographic films.

At one point, I just became sick of this kind of life. I was searching for a new life, for a way to escape all of these problems. As problems were mounting day by day, I started thinking of suicide, but I did not have the guts to do anything like that. When I told a Muslim friend of mine all of these problems, he suggested that I go with him to the mosque, and so I did.

That night, when I left the mosque, I brought a copy of the Qur'an home with me. Reading it just made me depressed and I could not get anything out of it. When I told this to my friend, he told me that I should read it in Arabic. But Arabic was not my mother language and I did not speak it. I started taking Arabic classes, but it was so hard and I felt like this was just making the problem grow.

I accidentally got a Kurdish Qur'an, translated by the famous Kurdish poet, Hajar. It was just as empty and dead and boring (with respect) as the one in English was. I finally made my decision that I would not read it again as there is nothing I could gain. It could not solve my problems.

One day, I was with my girlfriend at a bookstore. I bought a book that just made me curious. It was called *Siddartha* by the German author, Herman Hesse. When I read that book, I started thinking about Buddhism since the book was based on Buddha's life. But I still felt like the answers weren't there and something was missing.

One day, I met a few people who told me about God's love and His mercy. It led to a lengthy discussion. When I was about to leave, I accepted a Bible and a tract. When I went home, I opened it and closed it, and then put it aside.

When I woke up, it was 4:30 in the morning. Whenever I get up that early, I get headaches and I become dizzy; but this time, I felt like I had been up all night and I did not feel sick at all.

To my surprise and shock, the tract that I was given the day before was on my chest. Still hard-headed, I told myself that all of this time I have been running from God. I would try to just read the Bible this time and see what it really had to say. As I opened it, I saw a verse where it was written, "Therefore if any man *be* in Christ, *he is* a new creature: old things are passed away; behold, all things are become new." (2 Corinthians 5:17). I thought to myself that all this time I have been looking for a new life and here it is being offered. I put my Bible down and went to the bathroom. I washed my face. I looked in the mirror and all of my disgusting life just felt like "an old thing". I could feel God's Holy Spirit. When I came back to my bedroom, the Holy Spirit just brought me to my knees and that morning at around 6 o'clock, I accepted Christ as my Savior.

When I went to school that morning, I felt like I had rockets under my shoes. I walked all around and I just couldn't feel my feet. I could not help smiling. God's presence was everywhere. For some of my addictions, I sought help. My grades in school improved big time. My relationship with my parents and sibling also improved. I owe all of this to Jesus Christ who demonstrated His love by dying on the cross so that I don't have to pay the consequences for my sin.

CHAPTER 2

Ibrahim's Dream

My supernatural dreams first began during primary school. I was in the habit of praying each night before sleep — praising Allah, thanking Him, and continually asking guidance from Him. It was 1987, and after some time of meditation and prayer, that Allah spoke to me in a dream.

I knew nothing about the content of the Bible, but what I saw was very similar to what is recorded in the book of Acts of the Injil:

They were looking intently up into the sky as he was going, when suddenly two men dressed in white stood beside them. "Ye men of Galilee, why stand ye gazing up into heaven? this same Jesus, which is taken up from you into heaven, shall so come in like manner as ye have seen him go into heaven." (Acts 1:10-11).

In this first dream I was surprised to see clouds gathering on top of a mountain. After the clouds gathered, two angels dressed in white robes stood on top of the mountain. Jesus was standing between the angels. He left the angels and came to where I stood watching. As He approached me, I knelt down and He laid His Hands on my head. With the deep love I felt from Him, I began repenting. The dream was so powerful to me, but in the morning I told no one for fear of what my family may do to me. I remained silent for that year, telling no one what I had experienced.

A year later in 1988 I had another dream. Again Jesus was standing in between two angels at the mountain, but this time as He came toward me He was trying to go past me. I begged Him not to pass by me, and again I knelt down and repented. He did not lay His Hands upon me, and after I awoke I again remained silent because of my fear.

The third time came a year after the second (in 1989). As I looked upon the face of Jesus at the top of the mountain, he was full of compassion and smiling down upon me. The two angels were absent this time, but instead a vast multitude of people was present. We were going to where Jesus was, full of peace and joy. The next morning I sat down to meditate upon the most recent dream. After three years, I finally made an important decision to follow Jesus Who appeared to me these three times in such overwhelming love.

I again chose to remain silent about these events, but did begin to look for opportunities whereby I could get to know this Christ better. Ironically enough, the Gideons were distributing free Bibles at my school to every interested student. I received a Bible, the first one I had ever carried in my hands. Each student was encouraged to read it every day. The Lord spoke to me during that time as I read from the gospel of John:

Jesus answered, "I am the way, the truth, and the life: no man cometh unto the Father, but by me." (John 14:6).

This verse provided a bridge between me and Jesus, and I placed my full trust in Him.

CHAPTER 3

The Road From Damascus

Ziad was born and raised in Damascus, finishing his schooling in the historic capital of Syria. Most of his life, Ziad had been a practicing Muslim like everyone else in his devout family. He would often accompany his father, his three brothers, and some neighbors to the mosque for Friday noon prayers and frequently for prayer on other days. The rest of the five daily prayer times he would observe at home or at work. Not once had he failed to observe the month of fasting since his boyhood.

After graduating from the State University, Ziad moved to Riyadh, Saudi Arabia, where he worked for several years as a civil engineer. While he was in Saudi Arabia, he continued to participate in all the Muslim religious duties, as well as to make the pilgrimage to Mecca. At times he wondered about the Injil and the Tawrat, but he would brush these thoughts aside because he believed that through his traditional religious training, he knew all he needed to know about the Holy Bible and about Jesus Christ. Yet, according to his testimony, "what I had heard from my Christian friends in Damascus and had seen in their lives, rendered me unanswered questions for many years."

In 1979, Ziad, along with his wife and young daughter, Ghada, went to Germany for one year of specialized training as provided by his employer. During the family's stay in Germany, Ghada became very ill and was admitted to a hospital. After receiving medical care for four days with no improvement, the doctors seemed resigned to her imminent death.

Feeling overwhelmed by the scene of his daughter's pale face, Ziad left her room with a heavy heart, and returned to the waiting room. There he sat motionless, yet agonizing for a few moments, until he noticed a table in the middle of the room which contained books and magazines. He saw two recognizable books — an English version of the Holy Bible and a German version of it. He got up and walked over to the table and picked up one.

As he returned to his seat, he held the book closed while his memory took him back to some sayings of Jesus Christ which he had heard from his former Christian friends in Damascus. Recalling one saying, he eagerly opened the Book that was in his hand and directed by the Holy Spirit, began searching for the passage. When he found it, he began reading it silently:

"And whatsoever ye shall ask in my name, that will I do, that the Father may be glorified in the Son. If ye shall ask any thing in my name, I will do it." (John 14:13-14).

Seeing the willingness of the Son as expressed in these verses gave Ziad an abundant hope. He lifted a warm prayer to the Almighty God in the Name of

Jesus. His only request: that his dying daughter would be healed.

"Immediately I felt a profound tranquility and assurance," said Ziad. "I left the waiting room filled with unprecedented joy, seeing light surrounding me. As soon as I came into Ghada's room, I rushed to her bed and hugged her gently, saying, 'Ghada, my sweetheart, God will heal you.'"

The certainty with which Ziad made this statement even astonished him, but he knew deep in his heart that God had answered his prayer.

The tears which had dropped from his own eyes onto Ghada's cheek as he embraced her, Ziad wiped off. With tears of joy still clinging to his eyes, he turned to his wife and said, "I have asked God in the Name of Jesus to heal Ghada. Never before have I prayed so fervently, nor so simply in such a special way. Somehow I am assured that God has answered this prayer."

Indeed, Ghada was healed. Two days later, the doctors released her from the hospital. They could find no reason to detain her.

Since this amazing answer to Ziad's prayer, both Ziad and his wife have experienced the transforming work of God in their lives. They know the truth about Jesus Christ and proclaim their faith in Him. Later, Ghada followed them on this path; she too, now believes that Jesus is the Way, the Truth, and the Life.

Kind permission was given to share this testimony from Arabic Bible Outreach Ministry (www.arabicbible.com).

CHAPTER 4

Pakistani Muslim Comes Face to Face With Jesus Christ

I'm Azali and I'm from the Islamic Republic of Pakistan. I was an ardent follower of Mohammed until the results of a challenge I laid out before some Christian students. "And he said unto them, Go ye into all the world and preach the gospel to every creature." (Mark 16:15).

I belong to a Muslim family, and my parents forced me to learn the Quran by heart when I was seven, and so I did. When I was 14 years old I was studying in a convent school at Saddar Karachi, Pakistan. I had a lot of Christian fellows (or acquaintances) at school. I was surprised to see them studying, since I always found Christians in low profile in the society. I discussed and argued a lot with them about accuracy of the Quran and the rejection of the Bible by Allah in the Holy Quran. I always forced them to accept Islam. Often my Christian teacher told me not to do so. He said, "God may choose you as He chose the Apostle Paul." I asked them who Paul is; I know Muhammad only.

One day during our discussion I challenged them to burn the Holy Books of each other. They should burn the Quran and I should do the same with the Bible. We agreed: *The book which would burn would be false. The book, which would not burn, has the Truth in it. God Himself would save His Word.* Unfortunately they were not ready to do this, because they were frightened. Living in an Islamic country and doing such a thing could lead them to face the law and meet its consequences. I told them I would do this myself.

First, I set the Quran on fire and it burned before our eyes. Then, I tried to do the same with the Bible. As soon as I tried it, the Bible struck my chest and I fell on the ground. There was smoke all around my body. I was burning, but from a spiritual fire.

Suddenly I saw a man with golden hair, wrapped in light on my side. He placed his hand on my head and said to me *"You are my son and from now on you will preach the Gospel in your nation. Go! Your Lord is with you."*

Then I saw the stone on the grave, which was removed. Mary Magdalene spoke to who she thought was the gardener about taking the body of her Lord. The gardener was Jesus Himself. He kissed the hand of Mary and then I came to. I felt very strong, as if someone would strike me; I could not be hurt.

I went home and I told my parents about all what happened, but they did not believe it. They thought that the Christians placed me under magic; but I told them that all this happened before my very own eyes and that many people were watching this. They still did not believe and they turned me out of my home, and refused to accept me as their family member.

7

I went to a church close to my home; I told the Father there all about what happened. I asked him to show me the Bible. He gave me one and I read about the event of Mary Magdalene, and I accepted Jesus Christ as my Savior on February 17, 1985.

My family refused to accept me. I went to various churches and got more knowledge about the Word of God. I also followed many Bible Courses and then I started in ministry. Now after 20 years, I have seen many people come to the Lord and accept Jesus Christ as their Savior.

Thanks to the Lord, I am now married and have a Christian family. We are both involved in the work of the Lord and able to share the miracles God has been doing in our lives. Even though it is not easy and we face many hardships, we feel like Paul who went through hardships and suffering for the Glory of his Savior, who went Himself through suffering during His walk on earth and on the cross.

We thank God the Father for sending His Son to this earth and giving us free life through Him. We thank God for His Spirit who encourages us day by day to live for Him.

CHAPTER 5

Leah's Testimony

I became a Christian on July 21st, 1996. Let me tell you how this came about.

I was a very devoted Muslim but I began to feel that there was something missing in my faith as a Muslim. I started praying to God to show me if the Muslim faith was the truth, and soon after that I began to have strange dreams. In one of these dreams I saw some Christians standing in line to get into heaven. I tried to get into this line also, but a very tall being blocked my path and I started to cry. The side I was on was really horrible, but the side they were on was a beautiful place — so beautiful, so blue.

I could not get this dream out of my mind. It really haunted me. I confided to my Muslim friends about this dream, except that I didn't tell them it was Christians in the line in my dreams because I was scared of what they might think.

Well, they just said that God was telling me to pray more, and I did. But increasingly a great emptiness and depression enveloped me — emptiness like I had never experienced before. I couldn't sleep and I even started taking Ryhiphenol ("roofies") to get away from that feeling. I became a totally different person, a recluse, and started to seek out psychics, but it only became worse. I even wanted to commit suicide. I did not even fear death anymore.

Then, the day I told my best friend (who was an agnostic) that I was going to take my life, she said she remembered some Christian ladies who had come to see her a few times, and thought they might be able to help me. That same day, I met with them and they shared the gospel with me; they prayed for me, and that terrible emptiness began to lift and this huge load on me was taken off me. I started attending church with them and the second time I went, the pastor gave an invitation to receive Jesus Christ. I was so torn up inside. I fought the Holy Spirit and was trembling. I did not accept his invitation, but as I was walking out of the service, the Lord spoke to me: "It is now or never."

I broke down crying on the sidewalk and said to myself, I must go back to the prayer room where the people were getting prayed for to receive the Lord, and I did. God removed my burden and I started seeing everything in a new light.

Soon I began losing friends and all I loved and knew. Even so, God loves me and gave His Son for me, so that I would never perish. Incidentally, my best friend got saved the same day in a different church. The Lord showed me that I was truly on the right path.

I have never regretted becoming a Christian. It has been hard at times because I have been persecuted so much, but I have become even stronger in faith because of it. Right now I have a son who is being brought up as a Muslim. His father has denied me rights to communicate with him. I have surrendered my son to God because it has given me sleepless nights thinking of my son who is thousands of miles away from me and I have no control of what is happening now, but God is in control. Please pray for me and a miracle from God that I will one day be able to see my son again as we are now even living on different continents. I pray that this short testimony of mine will touch those who read it. God bless all of you.

CHAPTER 6

Tahir's Journey

My name is Tahir and this is my journey from Islam to Christianity.

Soon after arriving in the United States from Palestine 14 years ago, I married a nice Christian girl. She tried to become a Muslim to please me, but the more she did, the more I turned away from her. We had a child together, but the marriage didn't last because it is hard to love when your heart is filled with hate. Hate is what I was taught growing up in Palestine; hate towards the Jews, the Christians and hate against the world. As a Palestinian, you are taught from day one that the whole world is responsible for our misfortune, especially Jews and Christians.

After we divorced, my ex-wife told me that she had my daughter baptized. I was so angry that I stormed into the church, cursed at the priest who performed the baptism, and told him that he was going to hell because of it. I didn't want *my* child growing up Christian. My unsupervised visitation rights were taken away because my ex-wife feared that I would kidnap my daughter and take her to Palestine. The courts agreed and now I don't get to see her much anymore.

My next church experience was in college when a Muslim Arab girlfriend and I toyed with the idea of converting to Christianity just because it was a more lenient religion. We knew what we were doing was wrong and the punishment for apostasy in Islam is stoning, but we needed an ideology that would justify our sinful life. Because of an invitation from an Arab Christian girl from the college that we both were attending at that time, we visited her church one Sunday. The church service was full of joy, something I had never seen in Islam. After the service, a Bible and a book about the divinity of Christ were given to us. A few months later, and then again on Christmas Eve, we looked for a church that some Arab Christian friends from college told us about, but to our surprise it was closed.

My friend, Khalil, and I used to get together and talk about life and the state of the world. At times we wondered about Islam and why things are such a mess in Muslim countries. We wondered if this religion that we barely followed by tradition was for real. But our wondering didn't lead to immediate action.

I got married again. This time it was an arranged marriage with a girl from Palestine. This took place after my family stood in my way of marrying my college girlfriend due to the fact that she wasn't pure enough for them. I brought my new wife to the U.S. but found it hard to love her since I barely knew her. So, I was glad that my job took me from city to city. That way I could indulge in things unmentionable (including having girlfriends in every town) and not have to think about my situation.

Then September 11, 2001, happened. *As the towers collapsed, the last bit of respect I felt for Islam collapsed as well.* This catapulted me into an all-out search for Truth.

I was laid off from a very good job as the result of the economic fallout of 9-11. As I was online every day searching for jobs, "for some reason" I frequently landed in Christian chat rooms. One day I even found the Bible in Arabic online.

One late wintry night I found myself reading the gospel of John. I never trusted the Bible, and I was taught my whole life that the Bible is corrupt and has been changed. As I started to read, I was astonished. As I began reading about Jesus and his beautiful, pure, sinless, holy, amazing, miraculous life I couldn't stop. I remember reading the whole gospel from start to finish. It was early in the morning when I finished reading. I was crying so much that I was worried I might wake up my wife, and I didn't want her to see me crying so that she wouldn't ask me why.

A few days later, I logged on to my computer and "for some reason" looked for Arabic churches in the area. I then called one, and the voice on the other end of the line told me that his dad was the pastor, but he had passed away. He gave me another number to call a man named Farooq. This man is my current pastor and the person the Lord chose to lead me to Himself. We discussed deep issues like Muhammad's personality, lifestyle, his many marriages and his many wars. Farooq gave me a book he wrote that compares Islam with Christianity, complete with references from the Koran and the Bible.

As I began reading Farooq's book, I was both shocked and fascinated. I looked up the Biblical and Koranic references, all of which were actually there and couldn't believe my eyes! I realized I had been deceived all my life! The main issue that grabbed my attention was the completely different way the two religions treat women.

I can't pinpoint the exact day on which Farooq led me in a prayer accepting the Lord in my life as my personal Lord and Savior, but it was sometime in early 2002. I do remember the exact day I was baptized. It was the most incredible and scary day of my life! And I have changed so much since I accepted Christ.

I am free! I have found that there is *no* comparison between Christianity and Islam. Where I once had many rules to follow from the Koran and the Hadith, I now have a *relationship* with God. It's so different. Islam is based on force, but Christianity brings so much peace and love. I am a completely different man now. I am committed to my wife and am learning to love her. Now, instead of partying, I read the Bible. I attend church and Bible study when I can. And I don't hate Jews anymore.

I have been sharing my testimony and faith with pretty much anyone who comes my way. I shared it with my family, co-workers and even people on the street. It didn't go so well with my family, especially with my wife who still refuses to accept the fact that I have converted. She thinks that I'm toying with this and soon enough I would wake up and come back to my senses. My family, on the other hand, tried talking me out of it through debating about Christianity and Islam, then through abandonment and ignorance. But finally, they have come to accept me for who I have become, due to the good and loving relationship that we have. Were we still living back in Palestine, I'm sure things would be different and they would disown me or even try to threaten me.

By the way, my friend Khalil has also rejected Islam completely and refuses to obey its rules and commandments. He is living his life as a secular person away from religion altogether. I'm in continuous prayer for him to come to the Lord and get free from the evil one.

I gave my wife a copy of Farooq's book, but she was offended when she read it. Please pray for her to know the Truth. I want to go to church as a family, but this is only a dream unless she accepts Jesus. Currently, I attend Sunday morning church when conditions permit. My wife, knowing where I go, is constantly making up last minute plans to prevent me from going. I get most of my spiritual "feeding" through reading the Bible alone and listening to pastors on the radio while I'm in my car or online.

I wanted you to know what the Lord has done in my life. If you've been in America for any length of time, you understand that Christians aren't the big Satan, as you were taught. I am proof that a life can change when Christ sheds light in the darkness. I hope you will be challenged to see and learn more of the Truth, wherever it is found: radio, television, books, or online. May Jesus lead you in your search.

CHAPTER 7

Testimony of Farooq Ibrahim

I was raised in a typical Muslim family, where we would go to the mosque on Fridays and on special occasions; fast for the month of Ramadan; and celebrate the typical festive holidays of Islam. When I was a teenager, I completed the recitation of the Quran; and that in essence was a confirmation of the duty of a Muslim youth. Later, in my teen years, I was not satisfied with just reciting the Quran in Arabic — a language I could only read, but not comprehend. Therefore, my father got me a Study Quran by Abdullah Yusuf Ali and also a copy of the Sahih Bukhari Hadith collection. I studied them for a short while during my late teen years.

After I finished my twelfth year of schooling, I started studying engineering at an Engineering College in Karachi, but desired to study in the United States. My desire was to go to one of the best engineering universities in the U.S. I had aspirations to do wonderful things for my people and country. Unfortunately, I was not admitted to my first choice of engineering university. Then in August of 1973, I came to the U.S. and started in a community college. I lived a typical life in the States, spending time in getting my education and holding onto part-time or full-time jobs so that I could afford to put myself through college. My parents who were still in Pakistan helped, but there was not enough money to support the family and my education here. After a short while, I got plugged back into the local Islamic community and was involved with other Muslims in the study of the Quran and Hadith and their applicability in the local culture.

After getting my 2-year Associates Degree from a community college, God in His mercy and grace provided for me to get into my choice of engineering university as a transfer student with an academic scholarship. By the time I had completed my Bachelor of Science degree, I had veered away from the daily practice of my faith, and focused my life's interest in the academic and secular things in life. After working for a short while to gain experience and decide what I wanted to do for further studies, I chose to get my Master of Science degree.

Once in the work place, I started doing what most typical men do in the U.S. culture — start planning and working my way to the top of the corporate and financial ladder. I married a woman who had grown up in the States, had children, and life was typical and stressful. My eyes were focused on making a name for myself and getting all I could out of life. My earlier aspirations to do wonderful things for my people and country disappeared.

Then in March of 1987, I was in a bad accident and was very badly burned, while some others were killed. I had to take time away from work to recover. During this time, I had to face my mortality and deal with my blind ambition. I started to consider what legacy I was going to leave behind, and where was I going to go when I die. I wondered if I was spared from death for a purpose. Being a Muslim I believed that I would end up in heaven; but because of my life being the way it was — not actively performing the duties of a Muslim — I feared that I may perhaps be penalized in hell for a while. I then started again looking into the Quran and Hadith and Islam to find answers. This time my zeal to know my faith was fueled with the knowledge that there had to be a purpose to life; I was spared and had been given a chance. I wanted to know this Quran — which I believed to be the revealed word of God for all eternity — and the Prophet of Islam and his life and teachings. By this time I was back on my feet, starting to go back to work; but now I decided to take a job in the company that required minimum travel, so I would be spending a lot more time closer to home and with my family. I adjusted my priorities, and side-stepped onto the slower track, away from the fast lane of the corporate world.

Later on during this time, I was challenged by my Christian friends that Jesus was the only way to heaven and that the Bible was the revealed and uncorrupted word of God. This challenge ignited an even greater zeal to study the Quran, Hadith and the life of Mohammad in order to prove Islam to be the true way, and Christianity to be a false hope with Jesus being merely a man and not God. My desire was also to teach my children about Islam and to raise them Muslim. I spent the next few months studying the Quran and comparing it to the Bible. I compared the lives of Jesus both in the Quran and the Bible. I also compared the life and teaching of Mohammad and that of Jesus. I checked into the early history of Islam and Christianity and the sad but unfortunate atrocities committed by both religions, and the reasons why. I also read articles by others who denied the existence of God.

I reached a point where I was not sure how to deal with some of the difficulties in the Bible that were very unclear such as:

- Why are there four books to present the "gospel" and not one, as the Quran teaches of one gospel?
- What was this issue of Sin and the need for shedding of blood and a Savior?
- How could Jesus be God and Man, and what was this concept of the Trinity?
- Did Jesus really die on the cross, and was He resurrected or not?
- How could followers of Jesus commit the atrocities that occurred during the crusades?

But also in my quest to use the Quran as my standard, and the teaching and life of Mohammad as a model for life, I had some significant difficulties, for example:

- I had to deal with the concept of "abrogation". Why would God reveal later verses in the Quran that supercede earlier verses? This seemed at odds with the nature of God.
- There were inconsistencies in the Quran. For example, one must face Jerusalem in prayer, and then later it's Mecca. How can fornication be sin, but sex with many slave women, who have no legal marriage status, is tolerated? Tolerance and peace are taught in early revelation, but the command to fight all unbelievers is later directed.
- The Quran was standardized, but why command the older versions to be burned? Why the need to banish all with no traces of edited versions?
- Why was there such unequal status between men and women in the areas of marriage, law, social etiquette, modesty, etc.?
- Why the harsh treatment of non-Muslims in the community, and the command to Jihad?

At this point, I reached a place in my study that I could no longer defend the faith of Islam as it was clearly at odds with issues of truth and character of God as depicted in both the Quran and the Bible. However, I just was not ready to walk away from Islam. Christianity had its own set of issues, most of which revolved around the person of Jesus. At this point, I recalled from my childhood knowing some of the tenets of the Indian religions such as Hinduism, Sikhism and Buddhism. In all of my study of life and the sciences, it had become clear to me that there was a great creator and designer who had formed the universe and us. So there was no point in venturing into the philosophy of the Indian religions. I found they provided no answers that were consistent internally within its own teaching and externally consistent with the world around us.

Even though I had issues with Islam, I believed that there was a Creator God that I could and should pray to for answers. For me this was the God of Abraham (Ibrahim). I felt "safe" to pray to the God of Abraham as Abraham is highly regarded as a patriarch of Muslim, Jewish and Christian faiths. So I ventured, that just as God had revealed the truth to Abraham, I would pray to this God to understand what was true and direct me on the right path. As I continued to regularly pray and meditate, I studied the passages in the Quran and the Bible on Mohammad and Jesus and reviewed books and articles by Muslim and Christian apologists.

Some weeks went by, as I prayed and reflected on Mohammad and Jesus. Finally, the evening of Good Friday of 1989, I was jogging and reflecting on the importance of this evening for Christians. Did Jesus really get crucified as taught by the Bible and some secular historians, or was it some big hoax as claimed by Islam? What was this Sin that required payment by blood? As I prayed, I sensed a burden lifted off of me. I looked up, as it felt like some heavy weight was gone. I then looked down, to see if I was still on the ground. There was no external evidence, but in my spirit there was a clear sense. This particular phrase came to life in me and occupied all my thoughts: "Jesus is Lord". I responded in my mind, but what about Sin and the Cross? Did Jesus die on the Cross? The response in my mind came back loud and clear - "Jesus is Lord." I asked again, but what about the Trinity and this concept of three persons and one God, and again, the response was "Jesus is Lord."

At this point, all that I had read in the gospel accounts of Jesus came together. It was as if a veil had been lifted. That is why the Jewish Council had condemned Him to death, because He claimed to be God — blasphemy; that is why this Jesus had authority to forgive sins; that is why He told the Pharisees that before Abraham, was I AM, etc. He truly is God. Now the same old words in the gospel that seemed to be vague about his deity, were suddenly crystal clear. Jesus is God. His crucifixion and resurrection were the ultimate calling card of this God-Man. It all started making sense, and I was at total peace accepting Jesus as Lord. At this point, I also realized it did not matter that for so many years I had been a Muslim, that my brothers, sisters and some of my best friends were Muslim; I now believed Jesus is Lord, and I would follow Him.

Soon thereafter I understood what had happened to me. Jesus talks about this topic as to his real identity and what people misbelieve about him in the gospel of Matthew 16:13-17: "When Jesus came into the coasts of Caesarea Philippi, he asked his disciples, saying, 'Whom do men say that I the Son of man am?' And they said, 'Some say that thou art John the Baptist: some, Elias; and others, Jeremias, or one of the prophets.' He saith unto them, 'But whom say ye that I am?' And Simon Peter answered and said, 'Thou art the Christ, the Son of the living God.' And Jesus answered and said unto him, 'Blessed art thou, Simon Barjona: for flesh and blood hath not revealed it unto thee, but my Father which is in heaven."

That has been the start of a journey, of getting to know my Lord Jesus better, accepting Him as my Savior and His full payment for my sins. My desire has been to live my life worthy of my Lord as He empowers me. My Muslim family did not accept me at first. They tried to convince me that I was wrong, while I tried to challenge them with the Truth of the gospel message. When they realized I was convinced of my faith in Jesus being God, I was considered an outcast. Some time elapsed after which my mom's desire to bring the family together was resolved by them respecting my faith. Over the years, the mutual respect has resulted in a closer bond between us, and they have also been kind, generous and supportive as a family. During these years I also developed some very close friendships with Christians who challenged me, as well as met some new ones once I got involved with a local church fellowship. I was welcomed as a brother. Also in the process, my character has changed over time. Some of the traits that He has exposed and dealt with in me include pride, arrogance, anger, selfishness, and control among other sinful traits. He continues to change me from inside out to be more loving and kind to all.

Today, over 15 years later, having further studied the Bible, the Quran and various books and articles on Christian and Muslim apologetics, and having discussed with many Muslims and Christians alike, I am sure of my faith in the Lord Jesus and continue to follow Him, even more than at that day He chose to reveal Himself to me and called me to Him.

This is the written testimony of Farooq Ibrahim and copyright of his testimony belongs to him.

CHAPTER 8

Gunjoa's Story:
"Where Will I Go After I Die?"

1. LACK OF ASSURANCE

My name is Gunjoa; I am African, 43 years old, married, and father of three children. I live in a country where more than 90% of the population is Muslim. Islam is the religion into which I was born. My father is a fervent student of the Quran, much of which he memorized at a young age. I myself was sent to the Quranic school when I was three years old. Later I alternated studies between the French academic school and Quranic school. The days I didn't go to French school, I went to study the Quran. As I grew up, my boyhood friends and I did many foolish things. But when I reached the age of 19 or 20, I began to take matters of religion more seriously. I would spend a lot of time thinking about paradise and hell, because I had been taught at a young age that these two places exist, and that after death, each person will end up in one place or the other depending on whether they did good or bad during their earthly existence. This is what I had been taught.

Consequently, I would ask myself the question: "Where will I go after I die?" This question followed me wherever I went. It troubled me continually. As a result, I became more faithful in my religious obligations: I prayed five times a day, attended the mosque on Friday, fasted during Ramadan, gave alms, etc. Each time I finished my ritual prayers, I would ask God to put me on the right path, because I continued to be troubled by the thought of facing hell after death. I questioned people who knew Islam better than I. But I never received a satisfying answer. All they could tell me each time I asked was that I simply needed to fulfill my religious duties, do more good than bad, and then leave the rest in the hands of God who determines my eternal destiny. They all told me the same thing: "No one can know in this life where they will go after they die. Only God knows!" But such a response did not in any way satisfy my heart. Inside of me there was nothing but turmoil. I had no peace as the same question continued to pop up in my mind: "Where will I go after I die?"

For three years while I lived in the capital city to pursue further studies, I lived among a particular sect of Muslims who believed that their marabout (religious leader) was Isa (Jesus) who will come back at the end of the world. They attributed to their marabout a certain number of miracles. I was impressed with their stories and I thought to myself: If their Jesus could do such miracles, the original Jesus must have been truly great! I desperately wanted to know what kind of miracles the first Jesus did. I thought, "Surely there can't be any harm in this!" This is what motivated me to know more about "the true Jesus." I should tell you that up to this point in my life I had never met any true disciples of Jesus Christ, nor had I ever read their book, the Bible.

After I successfully completed my studies and received my diploma, I returned to my native town with a clear objective: I would do some serious research and find a book that records the life, words and works of Jesus Christ. Thus, one morning I got up and went to pay a visit to some Catholics. In my country, back in those days when one spoke of Jesus, the Bible or Christians, we automatically thought "Catholic." (Today this tendency is changing.) So as I was saying, I went to visit them, but it wasn't there that I found what I was looking for. But as I was walking back home, God opened my eyes to notice a little library where I was privileged to meet some evangelical Christians for the first time in my life. I was 25 years old when I began to read the scriptures of the Bible for myself.

2. FROM THE PROPHETS TO JESUS

Now my research began to take on a whole new dimension. As a Muslim, I continued to pray to God to place me on the right path. This was because I still had not discovered a solution to the dilemma which would not leave my mind: "Where will I go after I die?" I had not yet found a solid, satisfying answer. People around me continued to say, "Only God knows. No one can know their eternal destiny." But I wanted to know *in this life* where I would go after I died! After nearly two years of research, of studying the Bible, of reading the testimonies of Christians who came out of Islam, and of discussions with Christians, God's answer to my question became clear to me. I surrendered to the evidence. Yes, I had discovered some wonderful things!

First of all, in the Old Testament scriptures of the Bible, I discovered that all the prophets had announced the coming of a Messiah. They were preparing mankind to receive this Savior of the world who would come at the time appointed by God. The prophets prophesied about the Messiah's miraculous birth, the place of His birth, the circumstances preceding and following His birth. They also foretold how He would be mistreated by the religious leaders of His own nation who would misunderstand Him and hate Him. The prophets also announced the Messiah's sufferings and how His enemies would plot to have Him put to death. They even described in detail the manner by which He would die. Most importantly, they told why the Messiah would allow Himself to be killed, refusing to save Himself even though He had the power to do so. Certain prophets also wrote of the Messiah's resurrection which would take place three days later.

In my research I discovered that from the very beginning, it was God's plan that the Messiah should pay the sin-penalty for the whole world, so that all those who believe in Him would not have to pay that penalty themselves. I learned that the penalty for sin is death and eternal separation from our perfect and righteous Creator who must punish all sin. But the Good News was that the sinless Messiah would come to fulfill the meaning of thousands of years of symbolical animal sacrifices. Prophets like Noah, Abraham, Moses, David, Solomon and Isaiah all offered up spotless lambs and rams to God as blood sacrifices to cover their sins. This was God's idea. It was also God's idea to send the Messiah who would offer up Himself as the Final Sacrifice — "as a Lamb led to the slaughter." (Isaiah 53:7). However, there was a distinction. The Messiah's sacrifice would not merely *cover* sin before God, it would *remove* sin's penalty for all who believe God and His way of salvation. In reading the New Testament (Injil) record about Jesus of Nazareth, I discovered that He is the One who perfectly fulfilled all these prophecies, and not someone else.

Next in my research, I discovered in the Bible that this "original Jesus" had provided a clear and uncompromising answer to my question: "Where will I go after I die?" Jesus' death and resurrection was God's answer to my question! Jesus said, "I am the way, the truth, and the life: no man cometh unto the Father, but by me. ...For the Son of man is come to seek and to save that which was lost. ...I am the good shepherd: the good shepherd giveth his life for the sheep. ...Verily, verily, I say unto you, He that heareth my word, and believeth on him that sent me, hath everlasting life, and shall not come into condemnation; but is passed from death unto life." (John 14:6; Luke 19:10; John 10:11; John 5:24). Such words and many others like them in the Bible are declarations which no other person has ever dared to make. These and other verses in the Bible helped me to understand and accept Jesus for who He is: the One and only Savior promised by God, who died and rose again to provide a perfect salvation for all who believe. Thus, I placed my faith in the Lord Jesus Christ and in the fact that He died for *me*, for *my* sins, in *my* place.

3. CHANGES MADE BY CHRIST
Interestingly, after I placed my confidence in the Lord Jesus and in what He did for me on the cross, I felt a peace that I had never before experienced. What a change! I no longer have any worries about my eternal destiny, because I know that Jesus has paid the full penalty for all my sins which condemned me. I am saved! I am now completely confident about where I will go after I die. I know that I will go to heaven, not because I am good, but because of God's grace, which has been provided through Jesus Christ. My faith in Jesus has changed my perspective on life. Now I seek to please God in all things, not because I have to, but because I want to. God has changed my heart. I am no longer afraid of anything or anyone. Of course, I am conscious of the power of the devil and demons, and of opposition from people, but I am absolutely convinced that the Lord Jesus is infinitely more powerful. He has proven Himself to me personally so many times. He controls and cares for me, my family and every aspect of my life.

21

4. OPPOSITION

Right after I believed God's message, it all seemed so clear and logical that I didn't anticipate the major trials and troubles that awaited me because of my new-found faith. But I quickly learned the reality of what Jesus told the people of Nazareth (the area where He grew up as a boy): "...A prophet is not without honour, save in his own country, and in his own house." (Matthew 13:57). Not only did my father, my uncle, my brothers and my friends do their best to make light of Jesus' death on the cross for our sins, but they also harassed me in a number of ways, finally excluding me from the family, putting me out of the house. It was painfully difficult for me to be rejected by my own family like this. It was not what I wanted. They are the ones who put me out, simply because of my faith in Christ. When folks speak of Islam as a religion of truth, peace and love, I ask myself how that can be if it cannot even tolerate those who sincerely believe in the One about whom all the prophets wrote?

By the grace of my Lord, I have overcome all these hostilities about which Jesus warned us. He said, "And ye shall be hated of all men for my name's sake. ...In the world ye shall have tribulation: but be of good cheer; I have overcome the world." (Luke 21:17; John 16:33). In all these circumstances, God has taken care of me and has taught me many important lessons which have been a necessary part of my own spiritual growth. I have now been walking with the Lord for 17 years. What a privilege! Also, God has graciously been using me as He desires in His service for His glory alone.

5. SERVANT OF CHRIST

It was in 1991 that the Lord first called me to serve Him in some new, specific ways. "Then shalt thou lay up gold as dust, and the gold of Ophir as the stones of the brooks. Yea, the Almighty shall be thy defense, and thou shalt have plenty of silver. For then shalt thou have thy delight in the Almighty, and shalt lift up thy face unto God. Thou shalt make thy prayer unto him, and he shall hear thee, and thou shalt pay thy vows. Thou shalt also decree a thing, and it shall be established unto thee: and the light shall shine upon thy ways." (Job 22:24-28). I accepted His call and by His grace I began to participate in various projects: translation of gospel literature in local languages; production and broadcast of radio programs, and involvement in special outreaches to large groups of people.

Recently, the Lord has expanded my direction and vision. My wife and I are convinced that the Lord has called us to carry out an itinerate ministry in our country. The Spirit of God continually directs us in this way. Our vision is to follow the example of our Lord Jesus Christ who "went throughout every city and village, preaching and shewing the glad tidings of the kingdom of God." (Luke 8:1).

CHAPTER 9

I Found God...
The Story of Noor Agha Logari

My name is Noor Agha Logari. When I was about 10 or 12 years old, I had questions about God. I grew up in a strict Muslim family. My father forced the boys in the family to go to the mosque and perform all the religious activities, because he was a close assistant to the mullah. He used to have the task of calling people (Azaan) for worship.

I was privileged to go to school, which was rare in our village. I became successful in my religious studies, because I could read and write. At age 16, I could read the Koran faster than the mullah could. Whenever there was a religious ceremony, I would be invited to read the Koran because I was fast and had a good reading voice. Moreover, I memorized many passages from the Koran, but I did not know the meaning of those passages because they were in Arabic. The mullah explained some of the surah (verses) but not every verse.

One surah, which struck me, was "Amato bellah", which says, "we believe in Allah and in the angels and in his books." I asked the mullah and my father what these books are and where they were. They replied that these are the four books that Muslims believe in, the Torah (Pentateuch), Zabur (Psalms), Injil (the Gospels), and the Koran. Then they told me that we don't need the first three books, because the Koran is the perfect and the last book. This answer did not satisfy my soul, and I desired to see those books and read them so that my belief in God could become perfect.

At age 27, my wife and I went to India as refugees. I needed to learn English. There I met Chandy Verghese, an ex-Indian missionary who had served the Lord in Afghanistan, and taught English to the Afghani people. I went to classes not only to learn English, but also because I had nothing to do at home. He started teaching me English and talking about Jesus.

Whenever I went to him, I would share my burdens with him. He would say, "God is good. He will take care of you. He sent Jesus, His Son to die for us on the cross, to take our sins and burdens." Such statements looked foolish to me and I thought that he must have been stupid. I believed in Jesus as a prophet. How could God have a son? How could He die on a cross? If He was the Son of God, why didn't He rescue Himself? Moreover, I was thinking why did that man talk in English about God? I learned that to speak about God you must be first of all Moslem, and secondly, you read the Koran in Arabic. I was taught that if anyone tries to read the Koran in a language other than Arabic, it's blasphemy.

Although I thought he was stupid, I kept going to see him because I found him a gentle and loving person. I noticed a peace in his heart. He invited me to stay after class. There were a few Christians who would come and sing praise songs and read the Bible together. I just observed, twice a week, for about five or six months. After a while, those songs kept coming to my mind. I started singing them in my heart, songs like, "This is the Day that the Lord Has Made", which I liked very much. As the time passed, I was more active in participating in those meetings. I started reading the Bible, singing, and praying.

I liked to pray to God because it comforted me since I was without hope, but there I could speak to God directly. I was a refugee. I had lost everything — my knowledge, my post, my family, my country, everything. These prayers helped comfort me.

After five or six months, my English teacher gave me a Bible in my own language. As I opened the Bible, I read the first few verses in the beginning of Genesis. It touched my heart. I wanted to continue reading. I took the Bible home and kept reading. The first few verses reflected my life as a human created by God. God created me beautiful, but something went wrong in my life and I was in darkness. I read that God created light and that light was for me to walk in. I couldn't stop reading. When I reached the Psalms, I sensed those Psalms of praise and intercessions were speaking to the need of my heart. I started praying just like those Psalms and I began praying in the Name of Jesus. When I reached the Gospels, I found Jesus was the only One without sin and He gave His life for me. I couldn't stop crying and pleading for forgiveness from God.

Meanwhile, I started attending another fellowship comprised of people from the Persian world. The preacher was Ezekiel Joshua, a South Indian pastor who preached in our own Dari language. He showed the Jesus movie. Whenever I listened to him, it spoke to my heart.

A year later, I was baptized. It was hard for me to say in my language that Jesus is my Lord and Savior.

I had a believing, fellow countryman Hussain Andaryas who helped me understand the depth of the Bible. He encouraged me a lot. I could understand him very well, because we were from the same background and we spoke the same language. Later, I received some foundational Bible teaching from him.

Meanwhile, I took the Essential Christians Foundations course in New Delhi. My faith grew and I started preaching the gospel over the radio in my own language (Dari), because I came to a conclusion that my people — all Afghans — need Jesus, the only One who can give them peace. I started sharing with my relatives and among my countrymen who were refugees with me. Later, I led in a fellowship group for my people. There were about 30-35 believers and non-believers, including children.

I wish every Afghan would take time to study the Bible and be open to God. The only truth about God is revealed in the Bible and Isaa Masih, Jesus Christ, who is the only way to heaven. Isaa not only brought the message of love and forgiveness, He Himself became the perfect sacrifice for forgiveness of all our sins. "...for there is no difference; For all have sinned, and come short of the glory of God". (Romans 3:22-23).

Isaa' (Jesus) birth, His sinless life, His death on the cross and His resurrection made Him to be the only one in the history of man to be followed. He said, "I am the way, the truth, and the life: no man cometh unto the Father, but by me." (John 14:6). In the Book of Acts 4:12, it is written, "Neither is there salvation in any other: for there is none other name under heaven given among men, whereby we must be saved."

Kind permission to share this testimony was given by www.Godsavedme.com.

CHAPTER 10

Jesus Christ is Lord

My name is Paul. I was born under a different name, Kashif, to a Pakistani family. From a young age I had a close relationship with the supernatural. At the age of two, in my grandmother's courtyard in Karachi, I saw a brilliant light in the sky, brighter than the sun. It pierced my soul like a laser beam, and I was helpless before who I now know was God.

Later as I grew to be five, in my room God visited me once again. He asked me a question. "Would you die for somebody?" He asked. I didn't know the answer, so I turned it around to Him. He told me that "yes" was the right answer. I accepted His word, and immediately sensed a deep peace and joy.

Then He asked me, "Would you die for anyone?" Same thing, I didn't know; He told me "yes." After a thought, I accepted this advice, and time disappeared as I entered eternity. I could have walked through the wall at that point and never looked back.

As I grew older, I was often sent to the basement for punishment to await my sentence. In these lonely times, I would say to God, "God, if I could be born a second time, I would not be so mean to others."

In Edmonton, at medical school, I lost all sense of right and wrong, as I plunged into a web of lust, perversion, drunkenness, drugs and pornography. From this, I descended into addiction and the occult, as I tried to "find myself." During this time, many people in Toronto, where I was taking time off from school, offered me answers — from a drug-pusher, to a Buddhist New Age group, to Satanists, to Hare Krishnas, to my cousin who wanted me to see a mullah.

Finally, at The Glass Buckette on St. Joseph and Younge, the Jazz nightclub/restaurant where I worked, there was a Christian who told me about Jesus. Well, I wasn't going to let anyone preach to me because I had all the answers at 22. I refuted his testimony that Jesus had helped him to stop smoking and drinking and doing perverted things, and publicly denounced him, the way any hot-blooded Muslim would do to a simple preachy-type. You've been there, I am sure.

But God is merciful in ways you would only know, if you believe what I am about to tell you.

One day, thinking to myself — "Well, Mohammed had a greater revelation than Jesus, but then came Joseph Smith and Baha'ullah. So, the pattern is a new revelation as the situation requires." I decided to find out what new spiritual message I could offer the world.

After meditating the way I knew all these men did, I sensed a presence at my right shoulder. It asked me permission to use my arm to write down a message. I thought, "Wow, I really am going to get the latest revelation," and it came into my arm. This is no lie, as God is my witness. It began to write, "Believe if you can believe, receive if you can receive..." I paused, and thought about it and let it continue. But soon it degenerated into a message of hate and revenge and violence. This was no message from God! Scared, I dropped the pen, and immediately sensed the spirit withdraw to a corner of a room. There it cowered, radiating hate and fear at me.

I fell on my knees and prayed: "God, if You are there, help me now!" As I was finishing this prayer, the telephone rang. It was the Christian from work. I let down my guard and asked him what to do. He told me to read the little red New Testament he had given to me. Only the revelation of John interested me, as I dismissed the miraculous answer to my prayer as possible coincidence. But the next one was good. In Revelation, the author talks of the number seven many times. Seven eyes of God, seven spirits of God, seven judgments of wrath, and so on. Seven is the number of perfection in creation, because in six days God created the heavens and the earth and on the seventh day He rested.

You will be as surprised as I was when I sat down to write out the budget for the last month's spending:

Oct:	
Bus Pass	67
Rent	290
Phone	90
Food	120
Drugs	180
Misc	30
Total	777

But still, I ran from the message.

In August, 1994, I began to read the New Testament for leisure, as one would read the comics. In it I sensed the character of Jesus, as being wholly good. He did so many things for people, and the things He said were true. I decided to follow Him as my teacher, but did not really believe the theology of Christianity.

In September after two year's absence from medicine, I resumed studies, but had an insatiable thirst for the Bible. Even Old Testament books like Leviticus, and Deuteronomy jumped off the page at me and put life into my soul as I digested the character of God. I had many questions like: "How could you prove the Bible was true," and "How can you prove all of the theology is true?" — but God bypassed all of that.

In November, I went on a camping weekend with Campus Crusade for

Christ. Saturday night, I asked my questions about the Bible and Jesus being God's Son, but was unsatisfied with the responses, which were faith ones, not intellectual. But after many hours of singing and talking, the night grew warm and friendly, and I was left alone with my friend Dani, talking until three o'clock.

At this time, the whole camp was silent, except for the soft knocks which fell upon the cabin door: knock-knock-knock-knock-knock-knock-knock. Seven knocks. My heart pounded as Dani answered the door. In my mind I had the thought, "Behold, I stand at the door and knock. If anyone hears my voice and opens the door I will come into him and sup with him and he with me." Jesus said this in Revelation 3:20.

"Is there anyone there?" I asked Dani.

"Nobody is there," she replied.

It must be one of the students, I thought, and went outside to confirm my suspicions. I searched all around the entrance, but found no one. Sitting down on a swing to think, I felt a peace come over me and I was a child again. Wanting to see what Dani was doing, I got up and walked to the doorway. She was standing framed in the doorway, and there was a glow shining out of her face — a soft light radiating from her very skin. This startled me, and I confronted God: "Oh, God help me!"

Dani calmed me down and explained this was a sign from God to help me believe. "Jesus died for your sins," she said. I believed, but did not want to give up control, because I was stubborn. We sat in silence for many minutes. Then came a scratching on the windowpane. Dani went outside to see what it was. It was a sphere of light, hovering in the air.

Later, as we stood in the doorway to go back to our sleeping quarters, she saw a figure walking across the field. It must have been God. Everyone else was sound asleep.

Sunday, back in the city, I lay fearfully in bed at midnight. I remembered the words, "…God resisteth the proud, but giveth grace unto the humble." (James 4:6). I then humbled myself and asked God to forgive me for ignoring all of His help to believe.

Suddenly a small light, like the sparkly light on birthday cakes of children, came out of thin air, two inches away from my forehead, and entered my brain: "Fizz-pop!" I had a deep peace like such as I had never had. My restless mind ceased. My doubts were relieved, my questions answered. I KNEW the Bible was true. But, I still could not understand the most basic Scriptures. I still had to receive my gift.

The next day, somebody was brought into my path to open my eyes to the prophecies in the Old Testament about Jesus, which were fulfilled hundreds, even thousands of years afterwards, by Jesus. For example, he showed me that His birthplace had been predicted to be Bethlehem, and His words, spoken in agony on the cross, "My God, my God why hast thou forsaken me?…," were written by David a thousand years before Jesus' punishment on the cross. (Psalm 22:1 and Matthew 27:46).

Having had this revelation, I confessed my sins, and received the gift of the Holy Spirit. He cleansed me of the pain my soul never even knew it had in its numbed state, and replaced it with the holy knowledge of its Creator, and more joy than can be contained in a human. I was born again.

After my conversion, the Lord allowed me to meet many Christians from a variety of fellowships. They are all a blessing. Also, by His grace, I attended a Bible College for one semester, and am believing for His help to pursue further studies. He has blessed me by taking care of all my needs, according to His mighty Word — material, social, and spiritual.

He is Lord par excellence. I was baptized in June of 1995, and I am seeing from day to day how He takes care of me. Glory to the Lord. But if you really want to be free, look to the cross, where Jesus was crucified so that all men could have peace with God.

Pride, which God hates, is saying, "I know everything I need to know." Humility, which is what every student of truth should practice, is saying, "Others know more than me. Humble yourself before God and He will lift you up."

CHAPTER 11

God Had Plans For Me

I was born in a small town in Algeria and into a family with six children. France occupied my native country. My parents were unschooled and were Muslims, so I was a Muslim by birth. I was told that as an infant, I was so sick the doctor gave me two days to live; but God had other plans for me. No, I did not die. At a very young age, my parents enrolled me in a religious school where I learned to memorize the Koran. As a family and individually, we suffered a lot under the French occupation. My father was jailed many times, even one time when my eldest brother was forced to leave home to serve in the French Army for mandatory service. My family spent several months without a provider. We were even forced to leave our hometown and move elsewhere.

One day during the Algerian civil war, while I was playing soccer with my friends, we were shot at. Many died but I only suffered a bullet wound. God had other plans for me. While at the hospital, I saw many people suffer and die daily and nightly. I was angry with God and Westerners. However, Algeria became independent and I was very happy. Still serious about my faith as a Muslim and now in high school, I began to devote more time to it. I was an example to many students.

Life without the French occupation settled in, yet things did not change. My country was free and so was I, but I was unhappy and felt a void in my life. Some people call it an identity crisis. Maybe it was an identity crisis but for me I needed to connect to that one missing thing or a person. I needed to understand why I was born, and when I die, where I will be. Slowly I became a nominal Muslim and later actually thought that God did not exist. I also joined a local communist underground student movement. While still in high school, I started reading, studying philosophers, and also drinking, smoking and doing shameful things too embarrassing to talk about. I felt confused and lost. My major was Mathematics, so naturally I read some writings by Blaise Pascal, a French mathematician. In his so-called *Pascal Wager*, Pascal talks about whether God is or God is not. Though Pascal argues from a gambling point of view, I was convinced that for me this was no gamble or coincidence. This latter fact increased my desire to seek God.

I finished school and came to the U.S. to further my studies. I was very skeptical of strangers because of the scars of the French occupation. But God had plans for me. God gave me a Christian host family who befriended me and invited me to their home and to their church. One day I heard Dr. Mark Hanna, a Christian Lebanese writer, speak about Jesus Christ. I was not receptive but heard new things about this Jesus from Nazareth.

Later, I learned that my mother died. I was very close to her and could not accept her sudden departure from my life. Having lost my mother and having failed in other areas of my life, I was hurting, miserable, tired and fed up. I wanted to end my life. As if someone was talking to me, words came to me saying, "You want to end your life, then consider it done and give your life up to Jesus." I heard and read in a Bible given to me, who Jesus is and what He did for me on the cross. Someone suggested I start reading from the book of John. I understood I was a sinner and needed God in my life. I turned to Jesus, believing He died for me, was buried, rose again and is seated at the right hand of the Father in heaven. I prayed, inviting Him into my life, and I received Him in my heart as my personal Savior and Lord.

I came to Chapter 6 of the book of Romans and realized I needed to be baptized. After receiving instructions in a class from an elder on communion and baptism, I was baptized by full immersion two weeks later. God did it all. It was all His doing and nothing I had done on my own except to seek Him, repent and accept His free gift of salvation.

You know, I did not fully realize what happened to me until I came across Ezekiel 36:25-27. It says, "Then will I sprinkle clean water upon you, and ye shall be clean: from all your filthiness, and from all your idols, will I cleanse you. A new heart also will I give you, and a new spirit will I put within you: and I will take away the stony heart out of your flesh, and I will give you an heart of flesh. And I will put my spirit within you, and cause you to walk in my statutes, and ye shall keep my judgments, and do them."

God also helped me deal with many other issues and things I could not understand on my own. Knowing who God is and who I am, my desire has been to live for Christ by loving Him, obeying Him and serving Him. It is my prayer to be used by Him. "Who will have all men to be saved, and to come unto the knowledge of the truth." (1 Timothy 2:4).

I also came across Jeremiah 29:11 where God says: "For I know the thoughts that I think toward you, saith the Lord, thoughts of peace, and not of evil, to give you an expected end." You see, He has given me hope and a future. He had plans for me. Friend, God has plans for you, too. My prayer for you is that you seek Him with all your heart. This is for your sake, not mine, and certainly not for God's sake. He is waiting for you.

Jesus says: "I am the way, the truth, and the life; no man cometh unto the Father, but by me." (John 14:6). The Bible says: "For all have sinned, and come short of the glory of God." (Romans 3:23). Jesus also says: "For God so loved the world, that he gave his only begotten Son, that whosoever believeth in him should not perish, but have everlasting life." (John 3:16).

I urge you to turn to God now and give your life to Him.

CHAPTER 12

In the Valley of Tears

I am Ibrahim, who for the sake of my family's security, go also by the nickname Timothy Abraham. I am a simple Egyptian from the Delta region. Farms surrounded me from every side with streams of the luxurious Nile River endowing life with fertility. I had a strong Islamic upbringing in my childhood, studying in the village shop for teaching the Quran (al-Kutaab). They taught me to fear God (Allah in Arabic) who created the heaven and the earth in six days. There was not a single reason to doubt a religion which emphasized fearing God, doing good work and living a moral life. The recitation of the Quran was meant to produce a sense of tranquility. I enjoyed the Sufi circle of worship as they adored the person of Muhammad. This was Abu-al-Azayem's group. I was searching for more closeness with Allah Almighty.

One evening around 7:00 p.m. in al-Mahatta mosque, having finished praying al-Maghrib prayer; I was introduced to Muhammad Imam and Sulleiman Kahwash. They were vitally influential in incorporating me into their group called The Muslim Brotherhood, i.e., al-Ikhwan al-Muslimin. They encouraged me to be a devout Muslim and fast on Monday and Thursday of every week and break the fast with them in the mosque where we ate bread, cheese, palm dates (tamr), and delicious salad. I diligently imitated every thing the Prophet Muhammad did, even the sitting posture of the Prophet as he was eating. They were so kind to me. They also saw in me the potential of being an eloquent speaker. Therefore, Sulleiman Hashem, the leader at the time, approached me gently saying, "Ibrahim, you are called by the Quran's teaching to proclaim the message of Islam "da'awah." *My Allah!* I pondered, *I am just 14 years old and I am easily intimidated.* Nevertheless, Sulleiman gave me a stack of books to study in preparation for the sermon I was to deliver the next day. From then on, it became customary for me to preach a sermon on the first Monday of every lunar month. I was filled with zeal as my leaders had arranged for me to go across the neighboring towns preaching from mosque to mosque.

I zealously wanted everyone to follow the tradition of the Prophet Muhammad, and subsequently, my sister had no choice but to obey my Quranic command and wear the veil which indicated modesty. I needed my father's approval. I wondered if he had ever heard his son, the 14-year old Muslim evangelist preach. To my astonishment my father was sharply criticized by people for having a son who was now a "fanatic." The Islamic Brotherhood was regarded as a religious gang by the majority of regular Muslims. My father, therefore, became wrathful over my Islamic radicalism and thoughtlessly punched me in the teeth. Today my front tooth is a fake one. It reminds me of my former perseverance to the point of death to be a zealous Muslim fundamentalist and my willingness to be persecuted for my commitment. My father burnt my Sunni (mostly wahabi and salafi) Islamic library. He knew quite well that Mohammad Mansour, a security police informer, was recording my sermons from the bathroom in the mosque. I was so strict in the fashion of the sunnah of Muhammad that I did not shake hands with women. I simply wanted to be a devout Muslim. Having finished their prayers in the mosque, my father stopped one of the leaders in my group, Sulleiman Hashem, and asked him pleadingly to leave me, his son, alone. When my father swore an oath of divorce (hilif alaya bi al-talaaq) that I will not be permitted to enter the mosque where the Islamic Brotherhood is praying, I obeyed my father, but asked for mercy in letting me hear their sermons while sitting outside the mosque.

I was never daunted by any of this and continued to preach Islam everyday in the morning parade (taboor as-sabah) as well as in every mosque where I went to teach. It never occurred to me for a second that Islam could be wrong. In my pursuit to propagate Islam everywhere, a magazine came into my hands which had pen pal addresses from the United States. I chose one at random and wrote, hoping to convert the man into Islam. I wrote to John from Pennsylvania, U.S.A., back and forth for two years, each trying to convert the other. I read every book I could get hold of to refute the Bible. To make things worse, I had no respect for the Bible as I put my feet and shoes on it, since the Quran taught me it was corrupt.

Then John surprised me by coming to visit me in my village. That was the first time I saw a real Christian. His sincerity, frankness, genuineness, and openness impressed me. John stayed with me for two months. He had an amazing prayer life which served as a model for me in my latter life. I did not know that Christians prayed until I saw a "living epistle" right in the middle of my house, a man from a far off land who became one of us and genuinely incarnated the love of Christ. John had an amazing prayer life; he prayed more than he talked, speaking the words of the Bible. I became jealous of John's intimacy with God and increased my recitations of the Quran.

Islam is a religion that has to be credited for teaching its followers to be virtuous, chaste, and benevolent. There is no doubt that Muhammad remains a genius in history. One has to note, also, that a Muslim may do as many good works as possible in this world; and on the Day of Judgment, God weighs the deeds of every individual in a "balance." The good deeds will be placed in one pan of the balance, and the evil deeds in the other. If the good deeds are heavier, then the believer will go to the paradise described in Quran as a place of sexual pleasure and frolicking with the wide-eyed huris (sura al-Waqia 56:20-23). However, Christ our Lord said, "For in the resurrection they neither marry, nor are given in marriage, but are as the angels of God in heaven."

(Matthew 22:30). My Muslim friend, according to Islam, if your evil deeds are heavier, you will be cast into the fires of hell. It looks like you would need to be only fifty-one percent good to get into paradise. Yet you remain absolutely unsure whether or not you are going to heaven. All you say, my Muslim friend, is "Only God Knows!" You hope for the mercy of Allah and hope that the angels or the Prophet will intercede for you in the last day, so you will be saved from hell.

I was like you, my Muslim sister or brother, right in the same boat until I knew that you can be absolutely sure of going to heaven. Tears well up in my eyes just to recall how lost I was and now that I am found. While trembling in tears, seeing the majesty of God, I rejoice to know that I have eternal life for certain.

God in the Bible is both just and merciful. His justice requires that everyone be punished in hell, for He is perfect 100 percent. No matter how hard we try to please God, we always fall short of His perfection. Our good works will not bring us closer to God. God saw our insufficiency, and decided to pay the penalty Himself. He sent His Word Isa Al Masih (Jesus Christ), who is absolutely sinless and faultless, to carry the punishment of our sins on the cross. What can you say to the Judge when He chooses to pay your penalty for you? The Bible says in John 3:16, "For God so loved the world, that he gave his only begotten Son, that whosoever believeth in him should not perish, but have everlasting life." It is because God loves us that He sent His Word, Jesus Christ, to die for us. Islam never grants us the assurance of going to heaven, but Christ absolutely does! Praise God! Thank you, my Lord, for sovereignly choosing to pay the price Yourself in the Person of Your incarnate Word, the Lord Jesus Christ, Who is the express revelation of the nature of Allah Almighty.

After John left, his influence stayed. I thought I would depress John by saying, "John, your visit made me a stronger Muslim in the faith and do not try to convert Muslims anymore." Yet John prevailed in his supplication and prayers. His intercessory prayer moved the Lord to wake me up in the middle of the night as I had no sleep or rest. Inner conflict reached its zenith. Restless, I reached out to my Bible and opened it at random. I found, "...Saul, Saul, why persecutest thou me?" (Acts 9:4). I remember one day in the heat of a debate between me and John, I made fun of the Bible and said, "John, your Bible is the most absurd thing! How can you believe the story of Saul who became Paul, the servant of the gospel?" John said, "The story is true, and that is why I am patient with you. You will be another Paul one day!" I replied, "John, you must be out of your mind to think for a second that I could leave the religion of all religions, Islam!" Reflecting on the words, "Saul, Saul ..." I said, "Lord! Me? Me persecute You? I did nothing to You in person ... I remember I turned in a female medical student to the police ... but I did nothing to You. Is it true that He who touched one of Your people touches the apple of Your eye?"

Islam denies the crucifixion of the Lord Jesus Christ because the Quran intended to deprive the Jew of the victory they claimed was theirs in Jesus' death. The Quran asserts that God put somebody who looked like Him on the cross in the place of Jesus. Now my Muslim friends, God is not in the business of fraud, because if He had wanted to deliver Jesus from the cross, He could have done it miraculously without having to deceive and put Jesus' likeness on someone else. This Quranic error is too blatant, and proves that the Quran has no divine origin. Moreover, the Quran is self-contradicting. While it claims that the Jews did not really kill Jesus, it also affirms very distinctly the reality of Jesus' death in the sura of the family of Imran (3):55, as it states in the first part of that verse:

When God said:
"OH JESUS, I SHALL CAUSE YOU TO DIE,
AND THEN I SHALL RAISE YOU UP TO ME."

My Muslim friend, my goal is not here to proselytize you, but to raise the ultimate questions: Who is Christ? Was He crucified? And how does this affect you? If the whole history of humanity revolves around Christ, then my entire life and existence should revolve around Him, too. Denying the cross of Christ is contradicting history itself. Muhammad himself is claimed in the Quran to have been urged by God, to refer to the People of the Book (the Jews and the Christians) if he is in doubt concerning the Quran:

"And if thou (Muhammad) art in doubt concerning that which we reveal unto thee, then ask those who read the Scripture (that was) before thee."
Sura Yunus 10:95

For the first time in my life, I began asking the question "why?", and challenged everything I took for granted. All postulates were critically examined. This got me into trouble in an authoritarian society. Questions, they say, fly in the face of Allah. Obey. That is all. In the Islamic Brotherhood, our motto was "samaana wa ataana," i.e. "we have heard and obeyed." After years of study, I came to two logical conclusions: The Bible is the inerrant Word of God, and Jesus is the Word of God. I began to see it was possible for Jesus to be God. Intellectually, I accepted all the claims of the Christian faith, but in my heart I still feared being struck dead for calling the Almighty God "My Father." I needed a miracle! The Bible teaches us that no one can say, "Jesus is Lord" except by the Holy Spirit. (1 Corinthians 12:3). No wonder every salvation experience is one of a miracle of birth out of death into eternal life!

From the depth of my heart, in the midst of inner conflict, I cried out to Allah even in the mosque: "Lord, show me the truth! Is it Jesus or Muhammad? Could it be that You are my Father? Show me the truth, and the truth You lead me to I will serve all my life whatever the cost may be!" I burst into tears since I knew the cost could be outrageously too high for a weak, thin person like me. For how could I afford to be cast out of my family and sleep on the streets like a homeless person? And what if my leaders in the Islamic

Brotherhood would find out about me? And what if they, in their Islamic righteousness and zeal, rush on to defend Islam and kill me? According to the Islamic religion, an apostate should be given a three-day opportunity to recant, and after that the infidel's blood is legitimately shed in the name of Allah! The words of the Prophet Muhammad kept ringing in my ear, "Any person (i.e., Muslim) who has changed his religion, kill him." This tradition has been narrated by AbuBakr, Uthman, Ali, Muadh ibn Jabal, and Khalid ibn Walid. Yet I persisted in asking God to guide me — *Guide me, O Thou great Jehovah, pilgrim through this barren land; I am weak, but Thou art mighty.*

One night Christ appeared to me in a dream and said with a tender sweet voice, "I love you!" I saw how obstinately I had resisted Him all these years and said to Him in tears, "I love You, too! I know You! You are eternal forever and ever." I woke up with tears all over my face filled with abundant joy, believing that Christ Himself touched both my mind and my heart, and I yielded. I was filled with great passion for Christ, jumping up and down, singing praises to His name and talking to Him day and night. I would not even sleep without God's inerrant Word, the Bible, next to my chest.

I experienced what a "spoiled child" of God would experience: God would give me anything I ask for in prayer. But then, the Lord wanted me to love Him and worship Him for His own sake and not for what I get from Him. I tried to keep my faith secret, so I was baptized secretly in a pastor's house.

Filled with the joy of salvation, I could not hide or deny Christ anymore. Therefore, when my childhood friend asked me if Christ was crucified, I answered, "Yes!" and explained why. He prayed with me to receive Christ. He was shaking and perspiring every time he prayed with me. He could see how mighty the Name of our Lord Jesus was. My former leaders in the Islamic fanatical group, desiring to know who the spearhead was, threatened to kill him if he would not tell them everything about my evangelism. Sadly, he betrayed me and I was beaten up in front of the mosque where I had formerly preached Islam zealously. In their sight I was a blasphemous infidel who deserved to be killed unless I would recant. They regarded my conversion as the most horrendous form of desecrating Islam and the Quran.

Since my secret conversion was now made public and Muslims plotted to kill me, I had to flee. I was hunted by Muslims from my village in the Delta to Ismailia, until I arrived in Cairo where my Christian friends lived; yet Christians were not willing to shelter me and I had to go back to the village, seeking refuge in His protective hands. I came back from Cairo and found an angry mob of Muslims filling up our house. My mother was wearing the garment of mourning, dressed in black, as is the custom in Egypt. To them by deserting Islam, I was dead!!! Muslim women yelled at me, "Your mother doesn't deserve all this from you. Why cause her all this grief?" Another woman lamented, "Poor mother! Her son left her for the Christian infidels. If I were her, I would kill my son for running after the infidels like a dog." I received a letter from a friend in Jordan who reported that my father was walking down the streets in Jordan weeping bitterly, as Muslim laborers there reproached him severely. He stayed sick in bed for a month because of this, until he and I talked on the phone.

It is absolutely unforgettable that outraged Muslims broke into our house barbarically. My mother knelt down at the feet of our neighbor Sayed, begging him to spare my life and kill her instead. In such indescribable agony, my mother disowned and disinherited me before all people in my village. I love my mother more dearly than any person in this world, but no human power regardless of how gigantic it is, can separate me from the love of Christ. I will always live for Jesus.

My Bible, all my Christian books, and music tapes were confiscated and burned. I decided to flee from the Delta region to Cairo. Even though the police were tracking me down, the Lord blinded their eyes and protected me. In Cairo, I was hiding at M.'s, an Egyptian Baptist friend who was comforting me all the time. I broke down when he read:

"And they departed from the presence of the council, rejoicing that they were counted worthy to suffer shame for his name."(Acts 5:41).

I am grateful to God for providing this friend, M., who discipled me, teaching me to live a victorious life rich in worship and thanksgiving. He gave me a pocket Arabic New Testament and told me frankly that his parents were afraid. Also, I was told that if they continued to hide me, they would be in jail forever. I had nowhere to go. So upon the advice of my secret pastor, I went back to the village, hiding the Arabic New Testament in my socks, praying that it would not fall out. I was eventually arrested and released repeatedly. I learned what it means to have God as my only Hiding Place. In prison, my Savior knows I have come to experience true peace. I was not shaken because I saw Christ in prison, not myself. I sang songs of joy in the midst of tears, anticipating the shining Morning Star to come and deliver me. I decided to hide the Bible in a place where the police could not confiscate it — in my heart by memorizing it. I have since made it a habit to sleep with my Bible by my side. Five years later, I managed to flee Muslims' attempts to kill me and I was shocked to find out that there are some professing Christians in America who attack the Bible for which I was willing to die. God's Word has given me promises of faith which I apply as a little child and pray them through in confidence. The gates of heaven open as we pray through God's Word. His Word speaks life!!!

Once when I went to give my mother a Mother's Day gift, she asked me rhetorically, "Mother's Day gift?" I answered, "Yes" every time she repeated the question. She looked at me with such crushing grief and said, "My son, whom I waited 15 years to have and finally was born is now dead. I disown you till the day of judgment, Ibrahim." I cried but Christ touched my heart and said, "I am your family now! I am your father, brother, mother, sister, friend, and everything to you, Timothy, now." I cannot forget those days when my mother would call the police to arrest me. She even went to a witch to put a curse on me and bring me back to the fold of Islam. The witch said, "Your son is following a path which he will never forsake and he will be victorious all his life as long as he walks in it." These words, from the mouth of a witch, brought my younger brother to know Christ. The testimony of demons, about our victorious Lord, renders skepticism and unbelief absurd. Apostle Paul says in Romans 8:35-39:

"Who shall separate us from the love of Christ? shall tribulation, or distress, or persecution, or famine, or nakedness, or peril, or sword? As it is written, For thy sake we are killed all the day long; we are accounted as sheep for the slaughter. Nay, in all these things we are more than conquerors through him that loved us. For I am persuaded, that neither death, nor life, nor angels, nor principalities, nor powers, nor things present, nor things to come, Nor height, nor depth, nor any other creature, shall be able to separate us from the love of God, which is in Christ Jesus our Lord."

You also can be more than a conqueror through Christ, your Victor who loves you! Believe it!

I lost my Bible and all my Christian books were confiscated. All I had was the radio. I went sneaking to get my radio to listen secretly to Voice of Hope, searching for some "comfort" songs in the night. (By the way, I speak now publicly over Voice of Hope since I live in a free country, America). Yet, my mother caught me and she immediately snatched the radio out of my hand and beat me on the head with her shoes. I was just 20 years old at that time. I prayed for a Bible and the Lord heard me. I went to pick up a Bible package from the post office. The head of the post office, Kamal, slapped me forcefully and punched me in the face. I saw all kinds of terror...I was crying from the intensity of pain. He said to me, "You just go after these Christian infidels, leave Islam and we will wipe you out. We will send you behind the sun!" I felt trapped praying fervently to leave Egypt and practice my faith in Christ.

Father of comfort, You never left me. Please remind me of Your Son hanging on the cross crying out in the depth of agony, "My God, my God why have You forsaken me?" Lord Jesus, they all forsook You, and yet You found rest in Your Father. I need to depend on the Father as You did.

After 3 years, I decided to move to Cairo which was not any safer. The last time the police had arrested me, they said, "According to us, you are an infidel who has committed high treason. Next time we arrest you, it will be capital punishment." To make it worse, the "Christian" landlord told me he could not shelter a fugitive criminal anymore. I was not welcome in my own country anymore. Nevertheless, the Lord intervened, and a Palestinian evangelist, Anis Shorrosh, introduced me to Dr. Paige Patterson. He began to help me apply for a visa to the United States. At first, I was denied the visa, but Dr. Patterson did not give up. Finally, I was granted an entry visa, and I was supernaturally able to leave Egypt.

Lord, You never deliver your children out of bondage to bring them back into it...Help me to live somewhere to practice my Christian faith without the police harassment. Lord, please do whatever it takes so I don't have to live in an environment where people would force me to go into the mosque. You want Your children to worship freely even if this means fleeing for their lives like me so that Christ becomes all in all.

If it had not been for Dr. Patterson, I would have been history today. I was scheduled to be executed, and God saw that He had more work for me to do. So, He used Dr. Patterson in supernaturally rescuing my life. God Almighty is a "Father of the Fatherless" (Psalm 68:5), and when my father and mother forsake me, as David declares, the Lord holds me to Himself. Is God the Almighty, Your heavenly "Father", my friend? (Galatians 4:6). God the Almighty and Majestic One "delights" in you personally (Proverbs 8:31).

Having fled to the United States, I was still afraid that I would have to face the Egyptian police authorities someday, especially in view of the fact that I came on a student visa, which could expire any day. According to the Egyptian government I am an infidel who has defamed Islam as well as caused national disunity. Allah alone knows how I have no hard feelings towards either Egypt, the motherland, or Islam. Preachers offered to hide me in ranches, if worse came to worse. I just wanted to live and not to be the scapegoat of somebody's religious wrath. One ministry organization sponsored me and sent a petition for my permanent residency. After six long years of waiting, the Lord honored my request by giving me permanent residence a few days before my wedding day, April 18, 1998. I did not want anybody to falsely accuse me that I married a woman so that I may get a green card. I have married Angela for her own sake, and not for the sake of getting a green card. I give Angela all of me, for the source of our love is divine. It is never a fleeting emotion, but a "covenant" in which the Lord is the "witness" between me and the wife of my youth, my partner and my best friend. (Malachi 2:14).

Here is the time for me to praise God for the gift of marriage. It is when I abandoned myself to God and the godly desire of marriage, that He brought along Angela. Angela is the angel of God to my heart. She is beautiful both internally and externally. We both share the same vision in manifesting the love of Christ to our Muslim brothers and sisters. I did not compromise for less than what I knew Allah wanted me to have: Angela is a woman of prayer, caring, affectionate, hospitable, giving and gregarious. She is perfect for me. I revel in the fact that she loves my parents and gives sacrificially to them. My prayer is — *Lord, what did I do to be treated with such extravagant kindness of Yours that You give me a wife who loves me and my family?* The Lord honored me for putting Him above my desire to have a wife, and now we are a praying couple. Indeed, our Creator and Redeemer is our ultimate Matchmaker.

Lord, may I never be secure or seek easiness in life at the expense of union with You. Didn't You tell us, Lord, "And ye shall be hated of all men for my name's sake: but he that shall endure unto the end, the same shall be saved." (Mark 13:13). Please don't let me rush Your salvation, Lord, in the midst of trouble, but please give me patience so I can endure hardships as a soldier of the cross of Christ! Lord, may Your love consume me to such an extent that the doing of Your will would be the real bread of my life. In Christ's Name, amen!

People may contact Ibrahim by email at JesusVictr@aol.com regarding any discussion or questions.

CHAPTER 13

My Personal Testimony – Akbar From India

My name is Akbar, son of Mohammed Khaja Mohinuddin and Navanbee. Here is my testimony. I'll share how I, being a Muslim, came to accept Jesus Christ as my Lord and Savior.

Before I share my testimony, I would like to quote a Scripture verse from the Epistle written by the Apostle Paul in Romans 10:20 where the Lord says, "…I was found of them that sought me not; I was made manifest unto them that asked not after me." The Apostle Paul quoted this Scripture from Isaiah 65:1. The reason why I quoted this verse is to testify how God, Who is gracious and loving, dealt according to this Scripture in my life and the lives of all my family. His Word has proven to be true, and it has been fulfilled in our lives. Though we did not seek Him, though we did not ask for Him, He found us and manifested Himself to us. Oh, I wish that each and every breath of mine could praise Him, and serve as a sweet song to my Lord Jesus Christ.

Here is my testimony. I am the sixth child to my parents; born on 4 April 1981 following three daughters and two sons in a Muslim family; belonging to the natives of Kesamudram, a big town in the Warangal District, one of the main districts of the Andhra Pradesh state in India.

My father was a conductor working for South Central Railways and my mother was a homemaker. My father was an active leader in the mosque, and my mother was a teacher of the Koran. They both were very passionate towards Islam and serious about following its traditions, rituals, beliefs, and teachings. My parents had brought us up in the same fear and faith of Islam.

It all started with my eldest brother. His name is Mustafa, born after my three elder sisters. Let me tell you how it happened. One day as he was walking on the road, suddenly he heard a voice calling him by name, "Mustafa, Mustafa, I am the Lord your God." He looked all around to find who was calling him but he could not find anyone except himself in that place. It was a strange experience to him, which had never happened in his life. Again, when the voice came the second time, he recognized it as coming from the sky. Though he realized the voice came from the sky, he did not know whose voice it was. Before he could think about anything else, he was surrounded by a power which was like electric power. It led him to a Christian tent meeting where a preacher was preaching about Jesus Christ. The power which was all around him said to my brother, "The one who spoke to you on the way is the same one that man is preaching about." My brother understood that it was Jesus Christ Who spoke to him. There he accepted Jesus Christ as Lord and Savior with strong conviction as the Holy Spirit dealt with his heart.

When my mother, father and all the family members came to know about my brother's new faith in Jesus Christ, they were very upset. We were Muslims. We do not believe that Jesus Christ is the Son of God. According to the Koran, He is just a prophet among many prophets. Allah does not have sons or daughters, and we do not believe in the crucifixion of Jesus Christ. Before the crucifixion of Jesus Christ, Allah took Him into heaven. Christians think He was crucified on a cross, as do Jews, but they crucified someone else whose face was changed into the likeness of Jesus Christ by Allah. We also believed that the Bible has been changed by Christians, and Jesus Christ came only to the Jews, and He promised that Mohammed would come as a messenger of Allah for the entire world. We had to follow Mohammed now.

My parents were very unhappy, and they were very angry with Mustafa. As the days went by, we had arguments and discussions between the Koran and the Bible. One day my mother's cousin came to visit us. She had been suffering with a hemorrhage disease for a long time, and became very weak because of continuous blood flow. She was expecting my mother to take her to a good doctor. My brother said, "I will pray for her." We accepted and watched as he laid hands on her and began to pray. She fell down and a screaming voice came out of her saying, "I will not leave her, I will not leave her." He knew from this that she was possessed by an evil spirit. My brother said, "In the Name of Jesus leave her." That evil spirit began shivering and left her saying, "Because of you I am leaving her, or else I would have killed her." After some time, she got up and asked us what had happened to her, and why she was on the floor. She did not know anything of what happened to her. All she knew was that she was healed. Healing, comfort and strength come into her body. There was no pain, no flow of blood. She was full of joy and a great glow of happiness was all over her face.

As this whole thing happened in front of my eyes, I started reasoning why an evil spirit left in the Name of Jesus, and why not in any other's prophet's name. Why did this evil spirit obey the command that was given in the Name of Jesus? What is there in the Name of Jesus Christ that even an evil spirit would obey Him? Why not in the name of Mohammed? What power does the Name of Jesus contain? My mind was filled with all kinds of thoughts and reasoning.

I decided to read the Bible to know more about Jesus Christ, Who was said to be the Son of God by Christians. With an open heart in search of truth, I started reading the Bible. As I was reading, I came across the Scripture in Mark 16:16-18 where in verse 17 Jesus Christ said, "And these signs shall follow them that believe: In my name shall they cast out devils; ..." This Scripture almost knocked me down and shook my spirit. This was spoken by Jesus Christ over 2000 years ago. I was amazed and felt awesome that the Word of Jesus Christ is true and still alive. His Word works and it had manifested before my eyes. His Words have life. According to this Scripture, when my brother commanded the evil spirit to leave in the Name of Jesus Christ, it left. I could not deny the fact that the Word of Jesus Christ is true. It had manifested before my eyes.

This incident had brought faith to me. If the Word of Jesus Christ had proven itself to be true in that instance, then all the Words of Jesus Christ in the Bible must be true. As I continued to read the Bible, I began to get answers to each and every doubt and misconception I had about Jesus. I got my answers to all the allegations made by the Muslims against Jesus Christ and the Christian doctrine. The Bible corrected me and helped me to understand that the Muslim theologians were wrong.

Through the Words of Jesus Christ, I was introduced to God, a loving father to Whom I could become close to. I could personally speak to Him and have fellowship with Him. God's love filled the emptiness in my spirit. I understood the love of God, and the purpose and plan of God through Jesus Christ, Who was sent to die on the cross to take away the sins of the world. John 3:16-17 says, "For God so loved the world that he gave his only begotten Son, that whosoever believeth in him should not perish, but have everlasting life. For God sent not his Son into the world to condemn the world; but that the world through him might be saved."

I understood that salvation is a free gift to all mankind through Jesus Christ from God, and that man cannot achieve it through good works. Philippians 2:8-11 says, "And being found in fashion [appearance] as a man, he humbled himself, and became obedient unto death, even the death of the cross. Wherefore God also hath highly exalted him, and given him a name which is above every name: that at the name of Jesus every knee should bow, of *things* in heaven and *things* in earth, and *things* under the earth; and *that* every tongue should confess that Jesus Christ is Lord, to the glory of God the Father."

On December 24, 1998, I accepted Jesus Christ as my Lord and Savior, and was baptized. Since then I've had a strong and passionate urge to preach the gospel and His Word of truth to a dying world. I left my job with a multi-national company, and I dedicated my life to preach the gospel of Jesus Christ and His Word of truth all over the world.

As the days went by, the news of my conversion spread over the town. It was embarrassing to my parents and all the relatives. It was considered shameful towards the family's name that my brother and I were following Christianity and preaching the gospel.

Gradually over time, members of my family began to accept the gospel, and came to Jesus Christ as the Lord miraculously opened their hearts as He opened the heart of Lydia in Acts 16:14 — "And a certain woman named Lydia, a seller of purple, of the city of Thyatira, which worshipped God, heard *us*: whose heart the Lord opened, that she attended unto the things which were spoken of Paul."

We have been excommunicated by Muslims from our region and from other relatives who were near and dear before. Being reproached for the Name of Jesus Christ, we esteemed ourselves to be blessed because He made us worthy to suffer shame for His Name. Although many times we've been threatened with death, we have never looked back. Whatever we have suffered, and are still suffering, is nothing when considering our Lord's love and crucifixion.

We have started a church ministry in our home town. We've preached the gospel of Jesus Christ throughout villages which are all around the town and district. I have worked with Campus Crusade for Christ. I took a Jesus film and projector, then went about evangelizing all around the villages, and even into deep forests where tribal people lived. I showed the Jesus film and preached the gospel. Many came to Jesus Christ and accepted Him as Lord and Savior. Church has been increasing day by day as many people have been joining. Right now the congregation of the church is more than 500-600 people. There are also many cell groups and branch churches in different places which my elder brother is looking after now.

Today, my family members are saved, baptized, and are actively participating in the ministry.

Recently, a few months back, the Lord led me to Mumbai to start a ministry, especially among Muslims. I shifted to Mumbai to start this ministry along with my wife Susan, whom I married recently.

Romans 10:20 says, "I was found of them that sought me not; I was made manifest unto them that asked not after me." Once again, this has been fulfilled in my life and the lives of my family.

Let all the glory and honor be unto God Almighty, Who is rich in His mercy and grace. Amen.

Akbar asked that I include his e-mail address: peterakbar@rediffmail.com.

CHAPTER 14

The Story of Zia Nodrat

In Kabul, Afghanistan, during 1964, a 14-year old boy, Zia Nodrat, enrolled in the NOOR Institute for the Blind. He already knew the whole Quran by heart. In Western terms that would be like an English speaker memorizing the complete New Testament in Greek, since Arabic was not Zia's mother tongue. He completed the six primary grades of the Institute in three years.

While attending his classes in Braille in the Institute for the Blind, Zia also mastered English. He did this by listening and repeating what he heard on a transistor radio. With the help of a small ear plug, he heard programs coming into Afghanistan from other countries. He eventually started asking questions about what he had heard, such as, "What do you mean by the substitutionary atonement?" He had heard such theological concepts during Christian radio broadcasts like the Voice of the Gospel coming from Addis Ababa in Ethiopia, Africa.

Finally, he shared with a few persons that he had received Jesus the Messiah as his personal Saviour. They asked him if he realized that he could be killed for this, since the Islamic Law of Apostasy for anyone leaving Islam is death. He answered, "I have counted the cost and am willing to die for the Messiah, since He has already died on the cross for me."

Zia then became the spiritual leader of the few Afghan Christians. In the Institute for the Blind in Kabul, the students elected him as the president of their association. But the next year after it was known that he had become a Christian, he lost the election for this position. One of his Christian teachers told him how sorry she was that he lost. He replied, quoting the prophet John the Baptist who said of Jesus, "He must increase, but I *must* decrease."(John 3:30). His goal in life was not to seek prominence for himself, but to be a humble servant of his Lord. Zia's father said that before he had entered the Institute for the Blind, he had been like a cold and unlit piece of charcoal. After his experience there, he had become like a red hot, brightly burning coal.

Once he borrowed the English Braille copy of the gospel of John. He opened it and read with his fingers. He then returned it and said that his question had been answered. When asked what his question was, he replied that in John 13:34 Jesus said, "A new commandment I give unto you, That ye love one another…" He wondered why the Lord Jesus called it "new," since the commandment "love thy neighbour as thyself" had already been given to Moses, as recorded in the Old Testament Book of Leviticus 19:18. But now he understood. He explained that until the incarnation of the Messiah, the world had never before seen love personified. He went on to state that the Bible reveals that God is love, and that Jesus as God in human flesh is love incarnate. This was what made the mandate new. Jesus said, "A new commandment I give unto you, That ye love one another; as I have loved you, that ye also love one another." In his perfect life Jesus has now given us a new model to follow.

Zia was the first blind student to attend regular sighted schools in Afghanistan. There he had a small recorder with which he taped everything his teachers said, so that he could go over it and learn it thoroughly. He thus became the number one student out of hundreds at his grade level. Those who failed in their classes were given a second chance to take examinations after the three month vacation. He studied the next year during this break and passed the tests. In this way he completed high school, finishing two grades each year.

Zia wanted to study Islamic Law so that he could defend Christians who might be persecuted for their faith. He therefore entered the University of Kabul, from which he graduated with his law degree. He also studied Calvin's Institutes on the side since he wanted to grasp the concepts of this Reformation leader.

The Christoffel Blind Mission in Germany gave the Institute for the Blind in Afghanistan an extensive library of Braille books in German. Since Zia wanted to read these, along with his other classes he went to the Goethe Institute in Kabul and learned German. As the top student there too, he won a scholarship to go to Germany to study advanced German. When the Germans found out that he was blind, they withdrew the fellowship since they did not have the arrangements or accommodations for a blind person. He asked them what he would have to do. They replied that he would have to travel alone and take care of himself. When he agreed to do that, they finally accepted him. While studying there with top students from Goethe Institutes around the world, he was number one in this advanced course as well.

Zia also translated the New Testament from Iranian Persian into his own Afghan Dari dialect. This was published by the Pakistan Bible Society in Lahore. Its third edition was published by the Cambridge University Press in England in 1989. He also traveled to Saudi Arabia where he won a memory contest on the Quran. The Muslim judges were so amazed and chagrined that a non-Arabic speaker had taken first space, that they also awarded another prize for the best Arab in the competition. Because different blind students like Zia had become Christians, in March of 1973 the Muslim government in Afghanistan sent a written order closing the two Institutes for the Blind, one of which was in Kabul and the other seven hundred miles to the west in Herat. All the expatriate teachers of the blind along with their families were ordered to leave Afghanistan within one week. As these dedicated teachers left, God gave them a promise from Isaiah 42:16, "And I will bring the blind by a way *that* they knew not; I will lead them in paths *that* they have not known: I will make darkness light before them, and crooked things straight. These things will I do unto them, and not forsake them."

The Muslim government then destroyed the Christian church building in Kabul, after previously having given permission to build it. President Eisenhower had requested permission for construction of this building from King Zahir Shah on his visit to Afghanistan in 1959, since a mosque had been built in Washington, D.C. for the Muslim diplomats there, and Christian diplomats and other Christians needed a place to worship on a reciprocal basis in Kabul. Christians from nations all around the world contributed toward its construction. At its dedication, the cornerstone carved in beautiful Afghan alabaster marble read: "To the glory of God 'Who loves us and has freed us from our sins by His blood' this building is dedicated as 'a house of prayer for all nations' in the reign of H.M. Zahir Shah, May 17, 1970 A.D., 'Jesus Christ Himself being the Chief Cornerstone'."

When troops arrived and started knocking down the wall between the street and the church property preparatory to destroying it, a German Christian businessman went to the mayor of Kabul, who had given the order, and said, "If your government touches that house of God, God will overthrow your government." This proved to be a prophecy. The mayor then sent a letter to the congregation ordering them to give the church for destruction, since that would mean that the government would not have to pay compensation. They replied that they could not give it to anyone since it did not belong to them. It had been dedicated to God. They also added that if the government took it and destroyed it, they would be answerable to God.

Police, workmen and bulldozers were sent to destroy the church. The congregation, instead of opposing, offered them tea and cookies. Christians all around the world prayed and many of them wrote letters to Afghan embassies in various nations. Billy Graham and other world Christian leaders signed a statement of concern and sent it to the King.

On July 17, 1973 the destruction of the church building was completed. That very night, the Afghan government that was responsible for the destruction was overthrown in a coup. Afghans who are quick to see omens in events say that Jesus the Messiah came down from heaven and overthrew the government because the government had overthrown His church. It had been a monarchy for 227 years. That night it became a republic, under President Daoud. In 1978 this government was toppled by a Communist coup, followed by the Russian invasion just after Christmas in 1979. Millions of Afghans had to flee their country as refugees. One of them was heard to say, "Ever since our government destroyed that Christian church, God has been judging our country."

Under the Communists, the Institute for the Blind in Kabul was reopened and Zia was put in charge. He did a fine job of reorganizing it. Then pressure was brought on him to join the Communist party. He refused. One official told him that if he did not join, he might be killed. He replied that he was not afraid to be killed and asked the Communist if he were ready to die.

47

Finally Zia was arrested on false charges and put in the Puli Charkhi political prison outside of Kabul, where thousands were executed. There was no heat in the jail to protect the prisoners from the cold winter weather. He had to sleep on the freezing mud floor in his overcoat. A prisoner next to him was trembling with cold since he did not even have a jacket. Zia knew John the Baptist had said, "He that hath two coats, let him impart to him that hath none…" (Luke 3:11). He took off his only coat and gave it to the neighbor. From then on, the Lord miraculously kept him warm every night. He slept as if he had a comforter over him.

In prison the Communists gave Zia shock treatments to try to brainwash him. The electric burns left scars on his head. But he did not give in. When he was offered the opportunity to study Russian in prison, he mastered this language also. The Communists finally freed him in December, 1985.

Following his release from prison Zia read Genesis 12:1-3, in his Braille Bible, "Now the Lord had said unto Abram, 'Get thee out of thy country, and from thy kindred, and from thy father's house, unto a land that I will shew thee: And I…will bless thee, … and thou shalt be a blessing: And I will bless them that bless thee, and curse him that curseth thee: and in thee shall all families of the earth be blessed." Zia felt God was calling him to leave Afghanistan to go as a missionary to Pakistan. He therefore got in touch with a friend, a blind beggar. He then dressed himself in rags. On their way out of the country, he let his friend do all the talking, thereby concealing his identity or detection from the soldiers. They thus were able to get through the Soviet check points along the main highway from Kabul. It took them twelve days to travel the 150 miles to the Khyber Pass and then on into Pakistan.

After Zia arrived in Pakistan, he was offered an opportunity to travel to the United States to study Hebrew since he was also working on a translation of the Old Testament into his Dari language. He declined, saying he had so much to do among the Afghan refugees that he could not leave. He started an Institute for the Blind for them. He learned the main language of Pakistan, Urdu, preaching in this language in Christian churches. He furthermore completed a book of New Testament stories in Dari for children.

On March 23, 1988, Zia was kidnapped by a fanatical Muslim group, Hisbe Islami ("the Party of Islam") and was accused of being a CIA agent because he knew English. He was also accused of being a KGB or Khad spy because he knew Russian, and of being an apostate from Islam because he was a Christian. He was beaten for hours with rods. A sighted person can brace and flinch when the blow comes. But a blind person cannot see the club coming and thus gets the full force, even like the torture the Lord Jesus Christ experienced when he was blindfolded and then struck (Luke 22:64). His wife and three daughters had been able to get out of Afghanistan and were with him in Pakistan at the time he was kidnapped. Soon after, his wife gave birth to a beautiful boy who looks much like his father. No one knows whether Zia ever heard that he had a son.

The latest word, though not absolutely definite, is that Hisbe Islami murdered Zia. Before he was kidnapped, he had told a friend that if this party ever captured him, they would kill him. This same party caught two Pakistani Christians taking relief items to needy Afghans, and tortured them. Before releasing them, one of the captors stated, "We are not going to kill you the way we killed Zia Nodrat." In addition, an Afghan news reporter on the Northwest Frontier of Pakistan claims to have evidence that Hisbe Islami murdered Zia in a cruel way.

The United Nations Universal Declaration of Human Rights in article 13 states, "Everyone shall have the right to freedom of thought, conscience and religion; freedom to manifest one's religion or belief." The story of Zia is a story of infringement of human rights. Zia has been denied his freedom and has probably been martyred for his faith. Before his capture, he asked a Christian friend to take care of his family if anything happened to him. The friend answered in the affirmative, not realizing that a short time later Zia would be kidnapped. He was able to arrange for Zia's wife and two of his children to be brought to North America.

God does not force a belief system upon people. He has given them liberty to choose. Therefore what right does an earthly regime or group have to impose a certain belief system? Our prayer is that the new government of Afghanistan will respect the freedom of religion which is basic to all other liberties. In Dari, which is the main Afghan language of Kabul, there is a popular Afghan proverb which substantiates this truth: "Isa'i badin khud, Musa'i badin khud." ("Let the followers of Jesus practice their religion, and the followers of Moses theirs.")

Jesus prophesied, "yea, the time cometh, that whosoever killeth you will think that he doeth God service." (John 16:2). After His resurrection, He commanded His followers, "...be thou faithful unto death, and I will give thee a crown of life." (Revelation 2:10). If Zia has been killed for the Messiah, he has gone on to his eternal reward. And all of like precious faith will one day see him again; as the Bible promises, "...and so shall we ever be with the Lord." (I Thessalonians 4:17). Then we will be able to learn the full story of Zia's dedicated life.

Permission was granted to share Zia's testimony by Fellowship of Faith, Toronto, Canada.

CHAPTER 15

Walid's Testimony

My name is Walid. I was born in Bethlehem, Israel. On the day that I was born it was one of the holiest days to Islam, the birthday of the Muslim prophet Mohammad (Al-Mauled Al-Nabawi). This was an honor to my father. For that, he named me Walid which relates to the Arabic word (Mauled) and in English (The Birth) to always remember the birthday of the Muslim prophet.

My father was a Palestinian Muslim who taught English and Islamic studies in the Holy Land. My mother was an American who married my father during his studies in the United States in the year of 1956.

Fearing the impact of the American way of life for their two children and while my mother was pregnant with me, my parents left to live in an area of Israel in 1960 which was called Jordan at that time. When they arrived in Bethlehem, I was born. As my father changed jobs, we moved to Saudi Arabia, then back to the Holy Land — this time, to the lowest place on earth, Jericho.

I cannot forget the first song I learned in school just before the Six Day War titled "Arabs Our Beloved and Jews Our Dogs." I used to wonder at that time who the Jews were, but with the rest of the kids, I repeated the words without any knowledge of their meaning.

As I grew up in the Holy Land, I lived through several battles between the Arabs and the Jews. The first battle (while we lived in Jericho) was the Six Day War, when the Jews captured old Jerusalem and the rest of Palestine. This was a great disappointment to Arabs and Muslims worldwide.

The American Council in Jerusalem came just before the war to evacuate all the Americans in the area. Since my mother was an American, they offered us assistance, but my father refused and turned them down because he loved his country. I still remember many things during the war — the noise of the bombing and shelling that went on day and night for six days, the looting of stores and houses by the Arabs in Jericho, and people running to cross the Jordan River from fear of the Israelis.

The war was called the Six Day War because it was won in six days, and on the seventh day a Rabbi by the name of Goren blew the ram's horn on the Wailing Wall in Jerusalem declaring the victory. Many Jews claim that this was a parallel to Joshua when he went around the walls of Jericho six times, then on the seventh day seven times; and on that day the priests blew the trumpets and everyone shouted with one voice and took the city. To my father in Jericho, it seemed that the walls had crumbled on him. During the war he was always listening to the Jordanian radio station. He used to say that the Arabs were winning the war, but he was listening to the wrong station. The Israeli station was announcing the truth of their soon coming victory. Instead my father chose to believe the Arabs who claimed that the Israelis were promoting propaganda.

Later on, we moved back to Bethlehem and my father enrolled us in an Anglican-Lutheran school since they had a better English course. My brother, sister and I were the only Muslims in the school. Being half Americans, teachers would beat us and students would laugh at us. When the Bible class started, I would leave the class and remained outside waiting. One day, I walked into the Bible class and the class 'bully' stood up to fight. He shouted, "We don't want this half American and Muslim to be here!" I refused to get out and the lady who was teaching the class asked me to sit down. Since then, I changed the school's policy and for the first time, the school allowed a Muslim to study the Bible. For the next three years, I studied it despite all the mocking.

Later, my father transferred me to the government school where I grew in the faith of Islam. I was fed the idea that one day, a fulfillment of an ancient prophecy by the Muslim prophet Mohammed, would come to pass. This prophecy foretold a battle in which the Holy Land would be recaptured and the elimination of the Jews would take place in a massive slaughter.

This prophecy in fact is documented in Mohammed's *Book of Traditions* which states the following: "The day of judgment shall not come to pass until a tribe of Muslims defeat a tribe of Jews." (Narrated by Abu Hurairah, Sahih Muslim, Hadith #6985; Sahih al-Bukhari, Vol. 4, #177).

When Mohammed was asked of the place this would take place, he said "In Jerusalem and the surrounding nations."

During my youth, like my father, I was always tuned to Islam and what our Muslim teachers taught. Believing in Muhammed's prophecy, I offered my life to 'Jihad' or 'Holy War' as the only means to obtain either victory or martyrdom. In Islam, martyrdom is the only way you can ensure salvation and enter into heaven, especially since Allah and his prophet Mohammed promised it. As the Quran states it: "Do not think of whom are killed for the cause of Allah (in a Holy War), to be dead but living with their Lord receiving his blessing". — Sura: The Family of 'Imran ('Al-'Imran, verse 169).

During school riots against what we called the Israeli occupation, I would prepare speeches, slogans, and write anti-Israeli graffiti in an effort to provoke students to throw rocks at the armed Israeli soldiers. We shouted, "No peace or negotiations with the enemy! Our blood and our souls we sacrifice to Arafat! Our blood and our souls we sacrifice to Palestine!" and "Death to the Zionists!"

I vowed to fight my Jewish enemy believing that I was doing God's will on earth. I remained true to my word as I participated in many riots against the Israeli army, always trying to inflict harm to them by all means and methods I could devise. I would start and participate in any riot I could initiate: in schools, streets, and even on the holiest place (the Temple Mount site) in Jerusalem called by Arabs, Al-Masjid Al-Aqsa. All through high school I would always be one of the first to provoke a riot.

Many others got involved in terror tactics against the Jews using bombs and armed assaults on Jews in an attempt to force them to leave Israel, but they never could pluck them out.

Nothing could change my heart, I could only die or a miracle needed to happen. The simplest way to describe myself is that I was one of those viewed on CNN throwing rocks and Molotov cocktails in the days of the Intifada or 'The Uprising'. I was one of those whom Jews would call a terrorist. The interesting thing is that I was not only terrorizing but I was terrorized by my beliefs which required me to gain enough merit and good deeds to go to heaven. But I never was sure if my good deeds would outweigh my bad deeds on the scale when I would be judged by God. Of course to die fighting the Jews would ease Allah's anger towards my sin and I would then be secured a good spot in heaven with beautiful wide-eyed women to fulfill my most intimate desires. Either way, I won and terror was the only way.

I remember one time in Bethlehem when all viewers clapped their hands with joy in a jam-packed theater watching the movie, *21 Days in Munich*. The moment we saw the Palestinians throwing grenades into the helicopter killing the Israeli athletes, hundreds of viewers yelled, "Allahu akbar!" (Allah is the greatest). This is the slogan of joy used by Muslims for victorious events.

I remember students used to ask the teacher during our Islamic studies in Bethlehem High School if it was permitted for Muslims to rape the Jewish women after we defeated them. His response was, "The women captured in battle have no choice in this matter, they are concubines and they need to obey their masters; having sex with slave captives is not a 'matter of choice for slaves'". This in fact was written in the Koran, for it says: "Forbidden to you also are married women, except those who are in your hand as slaves, this is the law of Allah for you." — Sura: The Women (al-Nisa, verse 24).

And in a different verse the Koran says: "O prophet; we allowed thee thy wives to whom thou hast paid their dowries, and the slaves whom thy right hand possesseth out of the booty which Allah hath granted thee, and the daughters of thy uncle, and of thy maternal aunt, who fled with thee to Medina, and any believing woman who hath given herself up to the prophet, if the prophet desired to wed her, a privilege to thee above the rest of the faithful". — Sura: Confederates (al-Ahzab, verse 50).

We had no problem with Mohammed taking advantage of this privilege as he married 14 wives for himself and several slave girls from the booty he collected as a result of his victorious battles. We really never knew how many wives he had and that question was always a debatable issue to us. One of these wives was taken from his own adopted son Zaid, as Allah declared that she was given to the prophet while others were Jewish captives forced into slavery after Mohammed beheaded their husbands and families.

In an attempt to change the hearts of Palestinians, the Israeli TV station would show Holocaust documentaries. I would sit and watch, cheering the Germans, while I chewed on food. It was impossible for me to change my mind or heart concerning Jews, only a "heart transplant" would do that job.

They once took our school for a week to a Jewish camp on the coast of Eshdod to mingle us with other Jewish schools. That didn't work. On the contrary, every teacher who spoke to a Jew was mocked.

My mother, on the other hand, tried to teach me a different idea at home, that she called God's plan. She spoke to me about Bible prophecy; she said that the return of the Jews was pre-planned by God and had been fulfilled. This, to her, was God's miracle in our generation for the world to see, that "His will shall be done."

She also told me about many future events to be fulfilled in our generation which is surfacing every day now. She told me of false Messiahs and counterfeits; but all that had little effect, because my heart was set on fighting against the Jews.

My mother was influenced by an American missionary couple who she asked secretly to baptize her. When she refused to be baptized in a pond full of green algae, the missionary priest had to plead to the YMCA in Jerusalem to clear the pool of men, and my mother was then baptized. No one from our family knew.

Many times, my mother would take me on trips to several museums in Israel, and I fell in love with archeology. I was fascinated with it. In my many arguments with her, I would bluntly tell her that the Jews and Christians had corrupted the Bible. She responded by taking me to the Scroll Museum in Jerusalem and showed me the scroll of Isaiah, still intact. There was no one taking pictures of any Biblical errors to prove of any corruption and I could not respond to my mother.

I remember when I still tormented my mother by calling her an "infidel" and a damned American imperialist who claimed that Jesus was the Son of God. I'd show her the pictures in the newspaper of all the teenagers supposedly martyred as a result of violence, demanding that she answer. I hated her and always asked my father to divorce her and remarry a good Muslim woman.

I would even pose with a grim and sad face for the school picture, as if I knew that my turn to be in the paper as a martyr would be next. Many times I risked being killed during youth protests and clashes with the Israeli Army.

I lived in Israel during the Six Day War, the PLO resistance, the Jordanian Black September civil war, the bloody wars in Lebanon, and the war of Yom Kippur. With no hope to destroy Israel and all these losses, we still hoped for that one victory since that is all it would take to destroy them.

My parents worried a lot about me, since I got thrown in prison by the Israeli Army. My mother went to the American Council in Jerusalem to try to get me out. She was so stressed her hair started to fall out. In jail, I learned more about the art of terrorism and when I got out, I was more fanatical than before.

When I graduated from high school, my parents sent me to the United States to seek a higher education. Of course, I got involved with many anti-Israeli social and political events. I still remember my favorite sick joke I used to like to tell my friends — that I hated Hitler very much because he never got the job done, that is: he never finished the Jewish problem "once and for all".

With Hitler being my idol, and Mohammed my prophet, I went on with my life with little regard for Jews, Christians, or anyone who was not a Muslim. I believed that one day the whole world would submit to Islam and that the whole world owed the Palestinians for their losses in all the battles with Israel. I also believed that Jews were prophet-killers and that they had corrupted the Scriptures to serve their evil desires. This is what Muslims teach. They also teach that Mohammed is our only redeemer and God's favored prophet.

As I lived in America, I could not forget the hundreds of thousands of Muslims who died just in the last 20 years in Iran, Iraq, Kuwait, Syria, Jordan, Lebanon, Afghanistan and in every single Muslim nation. I had to get revenge for them and someone had to pay the price. Of course, there was no question in my mind that the Jews had to pay the penalty; somehow we always managed to twist things together and make it their fault. One day I fought with a man and struck his eye blind. I was so happy to learn that the man was a Jew.

I was fascinated with Islamic history and I learned that the Islamic prophet Mohammed extradited a Jewish tribe from Saudi Arabia and ordered the beheading of all the men from another tribe. The women were taken as concubines. I used to believe, as Islam taught, that only a Caliph (Islamic ruler) could rule the world. Islam is not a religion for one's personal and moral life, but a system of law and government to the whole world. If not achieved through peaceful means, it would have to wage war against all who did not submit to Islam. With one billion Muslims living today, I believed that it could happen.

I'll be honest, all my life I was terrified every time I read the Koran, because after every other verse, there were always threats of hell fire for this sin and that. All I wanted was to reach out to my Maker: to say I am sorry, forgive me, give me another chance. But I failed to keep count of all my sins and my good deeds; and I was sure that at the end, my sins would outweigh my good deeds. So, I lived my sinful life depending on the love and mercy of my Maker. I always wondered about my destiny. Lost in my fears and doubts, I really hated the idea of killing for my salvation; and in reality, I never had the heart to kill a rat! How then could I kill a Jew!

Sometime in 1992, I was fascinated when I read a book titled *Armageddon, Appointment with Destiny*, by Grant Jeffrey. Some of the things explained in this book had many detailed prophecies about Jesus: his birth, life, death and resurrection and the re-creation of the state of Israel. Many of these prophecies came to pass just as God put them down in the Bible! What also amazed me was to find out that the chances for a man to predict hundreds of historic events written hundreds and thousands of years before their occurrences are one in zillions. What is more fascinating is that the margin of error had to be zero, especially when the fulfillment of many of these prophecies was happening in my generation. This kind of evidence had to come from a divine origin; that origin had to be God Almighty.

The struggle began. I was puzzled. How could the Bible be a fake, and corrupted by the Jews, if the land I grew up in spoke and cried out, as thousands of pieces of archeological evidence surfaced from the land of Israel confirming the Bible? The book of Isaiah, discovered in the Qumran caves, was found by a Muslim, Muhammad Deib, from the town next to Bethlehem, while looking for a lost sheep. From that discovery, they found the rest of the Old Testament which matched the Old Testament Bible in our hands today. It contained hundreds of verses predicting the coming of Jesus Christ.

I had to read the Bible to know who Jesus really was, to find out for myself. God finally led me to get to the bottom line as I started reading what Jesus said: "I am Alpha and Omega, the beginning and the ending, saith the Lord, which is, and which was, and which is to come, the Almighty." (Revelation 1:8).

Christ also said to the Jews: "Verily, verily, I say unto you, Before Abraham was, I am." (John 8:58).

It amazed me to find similar claims between Jesus and Mohammed. These claims were serious, as Mohammed said: "I am the beginning of all creation and the last prophet."

Mohammed also said: I was a prophet of Allah while Adam was still being molded in clay."

Moreover, he claimed to be the intercessor for Muslims in the Day of Judgment; therefore by all of these, he claimed to be the world's last and final prophet and savior.

These things always puzzled me. If Mohammed claimed all that he claimed, then who was Jesus who claimed to be our Redeemer and Savior? That question troubled me a great deal. One of the two claims had to be a lie, if there were two redeemers; the redeemer had to be in association with God since God is the only Redeemer. Christ or Mohammed had to be the Redeemer and Intercessor for mankind. The Bible or the Koran had to be correct. One of them was pure gold and the other had to be a fake, but which one...?

Vowing to make a decision for "The Truth", I stayed up late many nights comparing many details between the Koran and the Bible. At some point during my study, I prayed saying: *God, You are the Creator of heaven and earth, the God of Abraham, Moses, and Jacob; You are the beginning and the end; You are 'The Truth', 'the only Truth', the Maker of the true Scripture, the one and only Word of God. I suffer to find Your truth; I want to do Your will in my life; I long for Your love and in the Name of 'The*

Truth' I ask. AMEN!!!

I wanted real gold and would not settle for an imitation. I had to scratch very hard to look beyond the surface of the world's plastic religions. I believed in the Koran as the word of God because it had modern scientific laws; and only a book with a divine origin could have scientific facts written a thousand years before their discovery. I spent a month using a computer program searching for scientific clues in the Bible. Every verse in the Koran that was a scientific miracle, that led me and millions of Muslims to believe in the Koran, was already in the Bible. Many stories in the Koran had serious errors and with my knowledge of history and archeology, I knew that the Koran had serious faults.

With many of these discoveries, my claim that the Koran was a miracle was in question. The Bible had all of its miracles hundreds and thousands of years before. My foundation shook and I felt the sinking sand under me. Even the nations mentioned by the prophet Ezekiel in Chapter 38, whom God would destroy — most of them were Muslim nations growing towards Islamic Fundamentalism today.

What also helped me was that God led me to discover, through my study of the Bible, hundreds of detailed and unique verses concerning prophecies fulfilled to the letter. No man has ever presented such detailed predictions of future events without having more errors than truth. God is the only one that holds the key to future events and only the Bible has the key, not the Koran which lacks those most important elements of "Salvation and Redemption". I knew at that moment that I would have to be a fool knowing all of this and continuing to worship a different god than the God of the Bible. I really thought with my prayer, that God will lead me to the Koran, but that was not the case with me. In fact, since it was the other way around, I had to give up my pride and be open-minded to truth.

God said in the Bible: "Remember the former things of old: for I *am* God, and *there is* none else; I *am* God, and *there is* none like me, Declaring the end from the beginning, and from ancient times *the things* that are not *yet* done, saying, My counsel shall stand, and I will do all my pleasure:" (Isaiah 46:9-10).

God not only foretold future events, but declared them and brought them to pass, unlike the Koran which simply used terror tactics to conform Muslims to believe. Since I did not believe that the Bible was corrupted, I spent many days searching the Bible for Mohammad, as he claimed to be in it, but never found him. If the Bible had been corrupted it had to have happened after the prophet Mohammed since the Koran always addressed the Bible that was 'between his hands' at his time. From that time until now, Muslims have failed to provide one single Bible from the face of the earth to prove the corruption; and not one historical or archeological evidence has been discovered to disprove the Bible.

Even the death of that Muslim prophet was different than the death of

Jesus, since Mohammed died on the lap of his favorite wife, Aisha, while Jesus died on the cross in order to redeem man's sins.

I felt sad that hundreds of millions of Muslims today live without ever hearing or being challenged with this kind of evidence. It was astonishing to me to find that Muslims and the rest of the world recognized three main religions that worship God, even though God said that He is One and His Word is One. I was blind, but with the Bible only, I began to see — I mean really SEE!!! With so much Biblical prophecy fulfilled —showing the return of Israel from the grave; and the attitudes of Muslims and the world towards Jews — the end time is near.

Man has never changed. He still kills his brother as Cain killed his brother, Abel. The only difference is that we don't behead and stab each other in battles as much as we used to. We simply wage chemical warfare to exterminate each other like bugs, as human life is becoming less and less valuable. I began to see that sin was the source of all man's problems; and that the devil was man's worst enemy, not the Jews, of whom Hitler exterminated 6 million less than 50 years ago. Ironically today, there are tons of literature being sold denying the incident even occurred. I wondered what would happen if a Hitler, or a Mehdi, or an Islamic Khalifa (Caliph) came to power and had what we have today with all these nuclear bombs capable of destroying earth seven times over. God led me to look at the world that I live in — especially with the evidence all around — and ask myself: Does the world today foolishly deny the Jewish Holocaust, even despite all the evidence? Why does most of the world today deny the Messianic claim of Christ and the accuracy of the Bible?

God opened my heart and mind and led me to see how people today deny all the proofs He has provided for us in His Word, adapting themselves to false forms of worship. The Lord began to show me the satanic influences which affected my way of thinking. Regardless of my Islamic background, I used to think these influences were from God.

I was led to a new view of the world and the meaning of life and saw the need for salvation. Today, we all can see man's goal for a world government waiting for the devil to be the king! "Babylon" is being revived from the grave to unite the world one more time; we have only changed its name to "The New World Order" when it should be called "The New Babylon". I started reading the Bible and began to wonder why Zechariah prophesied: "For I will gather all nations against Jerusalem to battle; and the city shall be taken, and the houses rifled, and the women ravished; ..." (Zechariah 14:2).

In Islam I was taught that the second coming of the Messiah was in Islamic prophecy. He was portrayed as the one to break the cross and kill the pig, which was another setup for Muslims to follow the "false" messiah, the Mehdi, the coming Antiochos Epiphinias.

Contrary to Mohammed's prophecy, the Bible prepares its readers with the knowledge that the outcome of the siege in the time of Jacob's trouble will not be the total annihilation of the Jews; but that Christ Himself will descend on the Mount of Olives for judgment as He fights the enemies of Israel. Unfortunately, it will be too late for repentance and redemption for non-believers.

The saddest part is that hatred towards Jews is not an old out-moded idea from the far past. Millions of Muslims today have the same sick idea that one day they will do the same to all Jews in the Holy Land as Mohammed did to the Jews in Saudi Arabia. In fact, the permission to kill Jews and Christians and to take their wives as concubines was engraved in the Islamic "Holy Koran", and is the main cause for the hatred of Jews by Muslims to this very day.

The word "Truth" was stuck in my heart day and night, pounding on my soul as I continued to compare the two books, and to finally conclude that the Bible could be proven beyond any shadow of a doubt to be true gold — not only by hundreds of ancient prophecies that came to pass, but by one ancient word created by God from the time of Jacob until our generation. For all who doubt, that word was and still is 'Israel'.

Israel's existence today, and the re-gathering of the Jews from ALL parts of the world, is an irrefutable proof that the Holy Bible is the true Word of God. God scattered them throughout the whole world and then re-gathered them again from ALL nations back to their original land, in fulfillment of His promises in the far past until our present. He said: "... and I will gather you from all the nations, and from all the places whither I have driven you, saith the Lord; and I will bring you again into the place whence I caused you to be carried away captive." (Jeremiah 29:14).

The true God has never changed; He is still the same. I also learned that my enemy, the Jews, were chosen by God to write God's Word and God's plan for salvation through Jesus the Messiah, the only Messiah and Redeemer for man. I also learned that Jesus, the man from my hometown, was a Jew and that even my hometown was Jewish 'Beth-Lechem', which means 'Home of the Bread', as He said: "...I am the bread of life: he that cometh to me shall never hunger; and he that believeth on me shall never thirst." (John 6:35).

Beth-Lechem was given its name before Jesus came to this world. Jesus was from the people of my enemy, the Jews. Yet, He died for my sin. I had never heard of an enemy who died for another enemy and loved him so much that he allowed Himself to be beaten, spat on, mocked and finally crucified. Would your enemy die for you? Yet He said: "...Love your enemies, bless them that curse you, do good to them that hate you, and pray for them which despitefully use you, and persecute you;" (Matthew 5:44).

The Truth was in front of my very eyes, knocking constantly on my heart, and wanting to come in. I called on The Truth and He answered; I was blind and sought the truth, and now I see. He knocked on my door and I opened it, and now He had set me free! Christ said: "...I am the way, the truth, and the life: no man cometh unto the Father, but by me." (John 14:6).

My way of thinking, my feelings, and my goals in life began to change. I began to feel for the Jewish people. All the hatred left me. The desire to see them hurt was no more a thing in my life. Now, I hurt for them and pray for peace for Jerusalem continually. Instead of laughing at images of the Holocaust on television, I weep for them. I am even ready to give my own life for them, as did my Lord. I say it despite the outpouring of hate that could come from my own fellow Arabs and Muslims.

Yes, I say it to the whole world, I love Jews. I love them because of their Messiah. I love them because they brought Light to the world and through them came the Light and the Truth; and for that I love Jews. I no longer despise them; and I know from the Bible that the Jews are God's chosen people to give light to Arabs and to the whole world, if we only allow them. For God made them a blessing to the world and we need to love and support them as God said to Abraham: "And I will bless them that bless thee, and curse him that curseth thee: and in thee shall all families of the earth be blessed." (Genesis 2:3).

Knowing the truth transferred my way of thinking from believing in Hitler to believing in Christ; from believing lies to knowing the truth; from being spiritually sick to being healed; from living in darkness to seeing the light; from being damned to being saved; from doubt to faith; from hate to love; and from evil works to God's grace through Christ. This transformation taught me that without the (true) Word of God, things could look good on the surface but in the core lies deception. I accepted Jesus, the Messiah who died for all of our sins, as my Lord and Savior; to Him I submit.

Jesus said: "Come unto me, all *ye* that labour and are heavy laden, and I will give you rest." (Matthew 11:28).

Thank you, Lord Jesus, for fulfilling your promise.

CHAPTER 16

My Choice Is To Serve Jesus Christ

Islam is the main religion, in fact, the state religion in my country. Our law is subject to the demands and teachings of Islam. But I, Suraj El-Din, am a traitor to Islam. I was born into a Muslim family and therefore knew nothing about Jesus Christ. I had many nominal Christian friends, and I asked one of them for a Bible. When I read it, I was surprised to find that God loves me and made a way to forgive my sins.

I learned that because Jesus Christ died on the cross, I could be saved and would not have to die for my sins. In studying Islam I had not found the way to know God. In studying the Bible, I found that only Jesus could satisfy my hunger for Him.

I decided to believe in Jesus Christ and follow Him. When I did that, my life changed in a very good way. I had peace for the first time. I was baptized and became a member of a church. Then I began to speak in many churches and among my friends about my new-found life in Jesus Christ.

One day in December 1981 I talked with some people in a taxi about Jesus Christ. They led me to believe they were open to hear about the Lord. When I left the taxi, they asked for the address of my church and said they would like to attend. I gave them the address, not knowing I had already been reported because of my Christian faith. That evening they came to the church, bringing the secret police with them. I was arrested without a warrant or any legal grounds.

When I arrived at the jail, one of the guards asked why I was there. When I told him it was because I was a Christian, he called the barber to shave my head. They kept me five days in solitary confinement, and I was not allowed to call my family or friends to tell them where I was. The guards beat me and said I could go free if I would renounce my faith in Jesus Christ. When I refused, the officials transferred me to the prison for the most dangerous criminals in the country. I was never given a trial by a court of law.

I was put in a small room in solitary confinement for the next eight months. Although it is a law that all prisoners should have two blankets, when I asked for covers they said, "No, you are a Christian. You will not get any covers." I slept on the rough cement floor, no bed, no blankets and this continued through the winter without even the basic necessities other prisoners were given. Despite the extreme cold, I had an open window in my room and no heating. I received one meal a day made of lentils.

The head of the prison told me not to speak with anyone, as he was afraid others would believe in Jesus Christ. When the guard saw me speak with anyone, he would slap me hard and push me. Once when I was speaking with another prisoner who asked for a Bible, the head of the prison beat me with a whip.

Many soldiers came to my door and said, "You are a very bad man. You are an infidel." The door to my room was closed all day except for a five-minute break to go to the rest room. The rest of the time I stayed alone in my room.

Other prisoners were allowed to leave their rooms freely from nine in the morning to four in the afternoon.

For a month and a half my family did not know where I was. When they asked for information, the police said they did not know. I made the acquaintance of a prisoner who was permitted to send letters out of the prison. He sent messages to my family and friends, telling them where I was. They came to the prison but were told I was not there.

My brother, an officer in the Army, asked the secret police to tell him where I was so he could visit me and try to get me to renounce my faith in Jesus Christ. After his visit they decided to let three members of my family come, but they forbade visits of any friends, thinking they would be Christians and would try to encourage me.

I was not allowed to have any money, although all the necessities such as hot water in the winter and extra food were acquired with bribes given to the guards. My friends wanted to give me food, money, and clothes, but the authorities refused. For two months I had only the clothes I had been wearing when arrested. Finally, my family was able to give me clothes and some food, and another prisoner who had extra privileges quietly gave me two covers. However, I still had no bed.

The secret police warned my family not to help me very much. They wanted to make things hard for me so I would give up my faith in Jesus Christ. Members of my family were afraid they would be killed.

Occasionally the secret police would send a man to ask, "Will you renounce your faith in Jesus Christ and be a good Muslim again?" They would try to tempt me with the offer of money and a car, my freedom, and a job with the secret police. I said, "No."

When the authorities realized I would not give up my faith in Jesus Christ, they decided, with no explanation, to let me out of prison on bail. The secret police told me not to go to any church, and said if they saw me in church they would arrest me again and kill me.

Muslim law requires that anyone who converts from Islam to another religion should be killed. If another Muslim were to kill me for any reason, the government would excuse him, and he would not be arrested or even punished. I am considered a traitor to Islam, deserving to be killed.

Kind permission was given to share this testimony from Arabic Bible Outreach Ministry (www.arabicbible.com).

CHAPTER 17

Christ Changed My Life

Unlike many, I (Sommer) had attended church as a child. This was only during the summer time, though, when I visited my mother's parents in the United States. I grew up in Kuwait with a Muslim father and a Christian mother.

Having a Muslim father required me to study Islam. I remember the confusion at such a young age. I thought Jesus died on the cross, but I had friends who strongly disputed this. We were only in primary (or elementary) school. By the time I was nine years old, I had a nice and pleasant Arabic tutor who was a Muslim. She helped me with my homework and took me on picnics and other trips with her family and neighbors. I thought of becoming a Muslim by the time I was eleven, and she was my tutor until the end of that year.

At age twelve and on I was in confusion again, but I decided that loving God was important. I was easily occupied by a good group of friends. Even in my later teen years I went to parties where there was dancing. My mother would always make sure that there was a parent at the party. Most of the time these parents were scared when I arrived, because I was female and Kuwaiti. I never got into trouble, as far as drinking or drugs or even sex. I felt like I was a pretty good person.

I finally found the truth when I had graduated from high school. This was the same year that Saddam Hussein invaded Kuwait. I was saddened and hurt by what was going on. I was in America with my family. I had friends who were stuck in the country and some of them were Palestinian and Jordanian. One of my Palestinian friends had to give up her jewelry and beautiful clothing, before leaving. I would cry every night feeling like I was in the same identity crisis that started when I was thirteen. Eventually, all of my friends made it safe through the Gulf War, but one of my Palestinian friends lost her father due to unhappiness of leaving Kuwait. Life was unfair; I became angry at everyone, especially at the journalists. I thought that once Kuwait was free, I would be happy again, but it was not true. It would never be the same. My friends were supposed to be my enemies, although they had nothing to do with Saddam. Some of my friends decided they were my enemies, but two stayed loyal. In all this mess, I asked God what was going on. I began to have a hate for people in general. I was no longer as nice as I was.

I was not a nice person and I was very lonely. However, God was not about to leave me in the dark. I was going to church, since I could easily do it in America. I was asking questions, but at the time, Christians got on my nerves. I felt like they were finding excuses for their sins by saying Jesus forgives. I decided I was not going to think about Christians or Muslims. I was going to compare the Quran and the Bible, and look at the men of these religions. Here was Muhammad, who said in the Quran that other men could only have four wives, but he was special, he could have more. As a female, I was also questioning the idea of virgins in heaven (the houri). If women went to heaven then why was nothing specific in the Quran about their rewards? And wine was acceptable in heaven but not on earth. Isn't what is wrong on earth still wrong in heaven?

Then I looked to Jesus and saw a man who was not self-serving, never married because He knew He would die soon, and also He loved His enemies. He even spoke to the dirtiest people, the prostitutes and the tax collectors. He even loved them and wanted to forgive them. I let this become personal and realized He forgave my dark and hateful heart. If He could do that, I had to forgive the Iraqi soldiers for our property damage. I was nineteen years old, when I accepted Jesus as Lord. However, it would take me another year to forgive Saddam Hussein.

The Holy Spirit worked in my heart, and taught me to love people, even with all of their problems. I thank the Lord for what I have been through, and I now know what God wanted. He did not want me to be a Christian just in name, or because of my mother or American culture. God wanted me to be His in truth and in love, no matter where I go. If you ever feel so hateful, that you think it would destroy your soul, turn to Jesus. It doesn't matter where you are from, or what you have done, He has come to save the world through His death and resurrection, not to condemn it. I can say that the Lord has blessed me with good friends, even though I have moved to three different cities in America due to my husband's work. Still, Jesus is the best friend anyone could have. If you don't know Him, you need to.

Kind permission was given to share this testimony from Arabic Bible Outreach Ministry (www.arabicbible.com).

CHAPTER 18

The Testimony of Garba Adamu

Assalamu alaikum. All thanks be to the Lord of the heavens, the earth and all creation. My name is Garba Adamu. My parents came from Katsina in northern Nigeria. I was born at Miango, near Jos in Plateau State. Writing this in 1982 I am fifty years old, but I cannot be certain for we reckoned by important events, not the calendar.

When I was three years old, before I could talk very well, I entered Koranic school, my only formal education. Little by little I learned to read and write the Arabic-like script of Hausa, my mother tongue. After thirteen years I finished learning to read the whole Koran and went to look for work at the large missionary compound nearby. I asked the man in charge if he would have a job for me, but he burst out laughing because I was a very small teenager. Thank God, I was given a job sweeping floors and washing dishes. My employer saw that worked well and after a while I learned how to cook European food. I was able to bake bread, cookies and cakes, in fact anything they wanted.

While I was still unmarried, one night I had a dream which was very special, yet frightening. I saw the heavens open and an angel from God coming down with a message held tight in both hands. He came before me and said, "God says to you, 'Take this message.'" With thanks, I took it in both hands. Right away, the angel ascended into heaven. I watched and saw a beautiful shining light. I was amazed. All this happened very quickly, in about one minute. In the morning, before I started work, I went to the office of my supervisor to tell her what had happened. Instead of telling me what the dream might mean, she did not take me seriously at all. At first I was very unhappy about this, but as time went by I began to forget about the dream.

I was very much involved in my Muslim way of life. I married and after some years I married a second wife from among my own Hausa people. The missionaries did not like to employ a man with two wives and I was dismissed from my job. I began to earn my living as a market trader selling cloth. In my spare time I taught myself to read and write Hausa in the Roman script, which had been introduced by the Europeans who found our own Arabic script too difficult. At that time no one else among the Hausa of my town could read and write the Roman script. I learned with the help of the Hausa newspaper.

Some Muslim preachers visited our town with the aim of establishing a branch of their Muslim Mission in our town. Being able to read and write I was made secretary of the Mission in our town. I was a zealous Muslim, so after a while I was made secretary for the Muslim Mission for the whole of our local government area. The state headquarters provided me with a motorbike. I was appointed to assist the local Iman then appointed to the state executive committee of the Muslim Mission. As my responsibilities had grown I was to be provided with a car for my work.

Then one day the local Christian pastor came and asked if I would help at their mission. They wanted someone to help teach Hausa to Europeans. It was only for six weeks. He asked me in such a way that I could not refuse, though I told the missionary lady in charge of the course that I wanted nothing to do with the Bible. In fact, if I so much as touched a Bible, I would wash my hands with soap and water.

But this lady, Miss Oliver was not bothered at all. In fact she even helped me with my religion. On Fridays she would arrange transport for me to go to the mosque. She never criticized my faith or my way of life, except when I failed in my Muslim responsibilities. If I was engrossed in my work, she would remind me it was time for prayer. When I said I was too busy, she asked if I feared God. That was the strongest possible rebuke to me.

We taught Hausa using the Roman script, but one day Miss Oliver showed me a booklet in the Arabic script. It was about Jesus Christ, Isa Almasihu. I read it and kept on reading it again and again. I heard a voice in my heart asking, "Why do I not want to read the Bible?" So I went to work the next day and asked Miss Oliver if I could read the Bible for the students at their morning prayers. Language School started with daily prayers. I had refused to take part. Now this lady and all the students were really pleased to have me take part with them. I had never come across a European woman with such a character, so easy to get along with, so kind and calm. Before long I remembered my dream of many years before. I told her and asked what it could mean. She was not angry with me but told me that it seemed that God had an important message for me. This explanation pleased me a great deal.

Miss Oliver was writing a book "Jesus, Son of Mary." She was using the Bible and the Koran, writing in Hausa for Muslims and Christians. She asked me to read and comment on what she had written. I was to check the language. She wanted to know if the book really got her message across. When I read her chapter on the Holy Trinity, she was especially interested to know if I understood what she had written. I said that I understood far more than she thought. I asked to pray, and prayed that God would remove the darkness from my understanding and show me His truth. I told Miss Oliver that I repented from my sin and trusted in Jesus Christ. Straight away I had a joy that I had never before experienced. I stopped my Muslim activities.

When the leaders of the Muslim Mission realized that I was no longer active in their work, they sent a letter calling me to attend. I neither went nor replied. My answer was according to our proverb, "Keeping silent gives a message." They wanted to know why I had stopped my Muslim work and was helping Christians instead. Using occult ways, they tried to stop me teaching. I would feel as if something was falling on top of me. I would break into a sweat and feel dizzy. The students would hold me, help me lie down, then fan me while they prayed for me.

I would be taken home to rest while the students kept on praying. After a while the evil that was being used against me was stopped. Later I heard that someone gave the Muslim Mission a tape of what I was teaching. Like Miss Oliver I had nothing derogatory to say about Islam, nor any fault to find with the customs of my own Hausa people. I believe that most have never heard the Gospel in a way that they can really understand. All too often the life of the messenger has spoiled the reception of the message.

Miss Oliver left Nigeria not long after I became a follower of Jesus Christ. I have continued in the faith, employed by a Nigerian church teaching Hausa to newcomers to the country.

This testimony was translated 8 May 1996 from Garba's testimony in the Hausa language by Graham Weeks.

CONCLUSION

This book shared important testimonies from the lives of some courageous people who made life-changing decisions. Their decisions changed their eternal destinies. If there is any doubt as to your eternal destiny or salvation, then today, I urge you to consider the following Scriptures.

"As it is written, There is none righteous, no, not one." (Romans 3:10).

"For all have sinned, and come short of the glory of God." (Romans 3:23).

"For the wages of sin is death; but the gift of God is eternal life through Jesus Christ our Lord." (Romans 6:23).

"For there is one God, and one mediator between God and men, the man Christ Jesus." (1 Timothy 2:5).

"That if thou shalt confess with thy mouth the Lord Jesus, and shalt believe in thine heart that God hath raised him from the dead, thou shalt be saved. For with the heart man believeth unto righteousness; and with the mouth confession is made unto salvation." (Romans 10:9-10).

Now, here is a Sinner's Prayer to receive Jesus as Lord and Savior. Please repeat the following prayer and mean it from your heart:

"Dear Heavenly Father, I come to You in the Name of the Lord Jesus Christ. I ask You to forgive me of all my sins. I accept Jesus as my Lord and Savior and believe in my heart that He died on the cross for my sins, and that You raised Him from the dead so that I could be in right standing with You. I now repent and confess Jesus as my Lord and Savior. I thank You for giving me eternal salvation and ask that You would help me in my Christian walk."

I strongly encourage you to read your Bible daily to get to know the Lord better, talk to God daily in prayer and find a church where the Bible is taught as the complete Word of God.

ENDNOTES

Introduction
1. John McClintock and James Strong, *Cyclopedia of Biblical, Theological, and Ecclesiastical Literature*, vol. 6 (Grand Rapids, MI.: Baker Book House, 1981 edition), p. 406.
2. H.A.R. Gibb and J.H. Kramers (editors), *Shorter Encyclopedia of Islam* (Ithaca, New York: Cornell University Press, 1965), p. 274.
3. Alfred Guillaume, *Islam* (Edinburgh: Penguin Books, 1954), pp. 24-25.
4. Robert Morey, *The Islamic Invasion* (Eugene, Oregon: Harvest House Publishers, 1992), pp. 85-86.
5. E.M. Wherry, *A Comprehensive Commentary on the Quran* (Osnabruck: Otto Zellar Verlag, 1973), p. 36.

COMPILED BY

Commander Michael H. Imhof, U.S. Navy (retired), was born in Fort Bragg, North Carolina and raised in Blasdell, New York. He attended the State University College of New York at Buffalo, where he received a Bachelor of Science degree. He was commissioned in 1973. After completing Basic Underwater Demolition/SEAL training in Coronado, California, Commander Imhof was assigned to SEAL Team TWO, and subsequent Naval Special Warfare and other type commands.

Commander Imhof, possessing a Naval Special Warfare designator, has served throughout the world in numerous positions. Assignments include Platoon Commander, Training Officer, Operations Officer, Staff Officer, Executive Officer and Commanding Officer. He also earned a Master's Degree in Administration from George Washington University and served as an instructor at the U.S. Naval Academy. His awards include Defense Meritorious Service Medal; Meritorious Service Medal with two Gold Stars in lieu of second and third awards; Joint Service Commendation Medal; Navy Commendation Medal with Gold Star in lieu of second award; United Nations Medal; and other service awards. Commander Imhof also worked in Afghanistan in support of the Department of State after his military career.

A military officer of strong Christian convictions, Commander Imhof is ready and willing to share his faith with all. He is convinced that the Bible is the authoritative and uncompromised Word of God and gives thanks for the wonderful blessings of God in his life and the lives of his family. He is an active member in his local church.

Previous books include *Lessons From Bible Characters*, *More Lessons From Bible Characters*, and *Walking With God* (*A Daily Devotional of Spiritual Truths in Poetic Form*).

To Order Additional Copies of this Book Please Contact:

Evangel Press
2000 Evangel Way
Nappanee, IN 46550
1-800-253-9315
www.evangelpress.com

VOLUME TWENTY-ONE

Book One
REGIME CHANGE AND THE COHERENCE
OF EUROPEAN GOVERNMENTS
Mark Irving Lichbach

Book Two
OUTCAST COUNTRIES IN THE WORLD COMMUNITY
Efraim Inbar

Book Three
THE POLITICS OF INDEBTED ECONOMIC GROWTH
John R. Freeman

THE POLITICS OF INDEBTED
ECONOMIC GROWTH

John R. Freeman

Volume 21
Book 3

MONOGRAPH SERIES IN WORLD AFFAIRS

Graduate School of International Studies
University of Denver
Denver, Colorado 80208

CF 1A
HJ
8899
.F73
1985

Library of Congress Cataloging in Publication Data

Freeman, John R., 1950—
  The politics of indebted economic growth.

  (Monograph series in world affairs; v. 21, bk. 3)
  Bibliography; p.
  1. Debts, External — Developing countries. 2. Debts, External —
Latin America. 3. Debts, External — Political aspects. 4. Economic
development. I. Title. II. Series.
HJ8899.F73 1985   336.3'435'091724   85-1138
ISBN 0-87940-078-1

© University of Denver (Colorado Seminary) 1985.
Printed in Taiwan.

ABOUT THE AUTHOR

John R. Freeman received his Ph.D. in Political Science from the University of Minnesota in 1978, and he now is a member of the faculty of that same institution. Before joining the Department of Political Science at the University of Minnesota he taught at the Massachusetts Institute of Technology and at the University of Missouri. Freeman currently serves on the Editorial Board of the *American Political Science Review* and on the Panel of Consultants of *Comparative Political Studies.* Among the journals in which his articles have appeared are: *The American Political Science Review, The American Journal of Political Science, The Canadian Journal of Political Science, Economic Development and Cultural Change, International Studies Quarterly, Comparative Political Studies, The Journal of Peace Research, Political Methodology, and The Journal of Conflict Resolution.* Freeman is presently at work on a book length manuscript on the politics of mixed economies; the empirical part of this project is supported by a grant from the National Science Foundation.

ACKNOWLEDGMENTS

*Earlier versions of this monograph were presented at the 1981 Annual Meeting of The American Political Science Association and at the Conference on International Stability and Cooperation, Spring Hill Conference Center, Minneapolis, MN, October 12-14, 1982. This research was supported, in part, by the National Science Foundation under grant number SES 8105841. The author gratefully acknowledges the comments of Hayward Alker, Sylvia Maxfield, Brian Smith, the referees and editor of the Monograph Series, and the editorial assistance of Mary Ellen Otis and Millie Van Wyke. (None of these individuals nor the National Science Foundation are responsible for the conclusions drawn herein.)

TABLE OF CONTENTS

The Politics of Indebted
Economic Growth

1

INTRODUCTION

For many years the Third World has relied on the First World for capital and technology. Initially this entailed reliance on direct foreign investment; multinational corporations were encouraged by their governments and by international agencies to exploit the resources of developing countries and, in some cases, to develop the modern sectors of Third World economies. In recent years, however, dependence on direct foreign investment has diminished, as many Third World countries have relied less on multinational corporations and more on externally financed, local enterprises. In turn, international lending institutions, especially commercial banks, have come to play an increasingly important role in channeling First World capital and technology to developing countries. One manifestation of the reliance on indirect foreign investment is the phenomenon of "indebted economic growth" when the expansion of national output is accompanied by a buildup of foreign debt to such an extent that external financial liabilities come to constitute a large, often increasing, share of national output.

How prevalent is the phenomenon of indebted economic growth? And what, if any, problems does it pose for borrowing countries and/or international lenders? Answers to these questions depend, to some extent, on the time frame and level of one's analysis. In the latter half of the 1970s, for example, the ratio of outstanding public, publicly guaranteed and nonguaranteed private external debt to gross domestic product (GDP) was roughly constant for non-oil developing countries (Brau, et al, 1983:4). In much of the 1970s, the real rate of growth in these countries' total debt outstanding was equivalent to the real rate of growth in their GDP, as well as to the real rate of growth in their exports (Abbott, 1981:343). The fact that external liabilities constituted a portion of Third World output was of little concern to borrowers or to lenders in this period. The Third World had augmented its output without taking

3

on a new (large) financial burden and, concomitantly, international financial institutions had made loans calculated to yield steady earnings. However, when the time frame is extended to 1973-1982, the relative magnitude of the Third World's financial obligations significantly increases: the ratio of debt to GDP grew from 22.4 to 35.8, while the ratio of debt to exports of goods and services increased from 115.4 to 143.6. The Third World experienced growth then, but it also has been assuming a growing financial burden; an increasingly large share of the Third World's output has been mortgaged to international financial institutions. That this trend cannot be sustained indefinitely is a source of much concern to both borrowers and lenders. [Gross National Product (GNP) is often a better indicator of capacity to service debts since, in many countries, remittances from nationals working abroad amount to a considerable sum (*World Bank Debt Tables,* December 1981:viii). Between 1971 and 1979 the ratio of disbursed debt outstanding as a percent of GNP for all non-oil developing countries increased from 16.4 to an estimated 22.4 (*World Bank Debt Tables,* November 1980:viii). Also, by the late 1970s there was a "rapid erosion in the proportion of net transfer of resources to the developing countries. In 1976 these amounted to 56 percent of gross disbursements. By 1979 the proportion had fallen to 36 percent. In other words, there was a reverse flow to the creditor countries of almost $17 billion, the amount by which service payments exceeded net transfers" (Abbott, 1981: 343).]

Indebted economic growth is more prevalent in some regions than others. The phenomenon simply doesn't occur in parts of Africa and Asia. For instance, in South Asia the ratio of outstanding disbursed public and public guaranteed debt to GNP rose for a time between 1975 and 1979 but eventually settled at approximately its original value of 16.7; and, between 1971 and 1980, this ratio *fell* from 16.8 to 14.7. The ratio of this same kind of debt to exports of goods and services fell from 335.8 in 1971 to 171.9 in 1979. The ratio was estimated to be almost 400 in 1980, however (*World Bank Debt Tables,* December 1981:205). (Note the use of debt/GNP ratios here. I have been unable to generate reliable debt/GDP ratios for this and other regions.)

In contrast, the relative magnitude of external liabilities rose steadily in other regions. The most noteworthy of these is Latin America, where the shift from direct to indirect foreign investment has been quite marked. Commercial banks and other private financial institutions have become principal sources of foreign funds. Countries have borrowed heavily in international capital markets to finance a wide range of investments. For instance, Bacha and Diaz-Alejandro (1982:13, 14, 23) report that direct foreign investment accounted for about one-third of all the externally supplied long-term resources in Latin America in 1960 but only one-sixth of these resources in 1978, the difference being more than made up by the indirect foreign investment of privately owned financial institutions. The same authors concluded that most of these funds were used for investment rather than "excessive" consumption.

Many of the Latin American borrowers have experienced rapid rates of growth. But these growth rates have been exceeded by the rates at which debts have accumulated: between 1971 and 1979 the ratio of outstanding disbursed public and publicly guaranteed debt to GNP gradually increased from 10.5 to 20.3; in 1980 it was estimated to be 18.8. According to the World Bank, the ratio of the same kind of debt to exports of all goods and services produced by Latin American countries increased from 92.4 to 104.3 in this period (*World Bank Debt Tables,* December 1981:119). At the end of 1981 Latin America accounted for 43 percent of the combined public, publicly guaranteed and private nonguaranteed debt of all non-oil developing countries and paid 57 percent of all these countries' debt service (Brau, et al., 1983:3).

Brazil and Mexico are the two most indebted countries in the Third World. In 1980 their combined debts equaled roughly half of U.S. bank capital (*Business Week,* 19 January 1981:90). Between 1976 and 1979 Mexico and Brazil ranked first and second, respectively, among all non-OPEC Eurocurrency bank creditors (Morgan Guaranty Trust, *World Financial Markets,* December 1979:10). And at the end of 1982 they ranked first and second, respectively, in terms of debt to commerical banks (Brau, et al., 1983: table 6). These countries' interest payment burdens also have consistently been the highest in the Third World (for example, see *World Financial Markets,* August 1982, which defines interest payment burden as external debt as a percent of exports of goods and services). Brazil's debt alone has represented as much as 30 percent of all non-oil developing country debt and over 38 percent of all such debt to private banks (*World Financial Markets,* January 1981:table 5). It is estimated that Brazilian debt has generated as much as one-third of Citibank's profits (*Numero: Revista De Economia Y Negocios,* 18 April 1982:11).

Both countries have histories of indebted economic growth; between 1967 and 1980 the ratio of disbursed and undisbursed public debt to GDP increased from about .14 to .22 in Brazil, and from about .11 to .21 in Mexico (see figure 3). In terms of public and publicly guaranteed disbursed debt to GNP, between 1971 and 1980 Brazil's ratio rose from 7.7 to 16.6; Mexico's ratio increased from 9.8 to 28.8 in 1977 and then fell to 20.6

in 1980 (*World Bank Debt Tables,* December 1981:127, 161). Not surprisingly, then, these and other Latin American countries' development strategies have been the object of much criticism and concern.

What explains the phenomenon of indebted economic growth? Should it be a source of concern? Is indebted economic growth evidence that ineffective or imprudent development strategies have been adopted by countries like those in Latin America?

Observers agree that international economic events are, in part, responsible for the fact that debts sometimes have grown faster than output. The internationalization of banking, coupled with the massive reallocation of resources to oil-exporting countries and concomitant decline in the demand for credit in Western economies, has led financial institutions to reassess the credit-worthiness of developing countries, especially those countries which, like Brazil and Mexico, have sought external financing for new investments. In this way, changes in international economic relations have resulted in more capital being made available from loans to Third World countries initially through an essentially unregulated set of (global) capital markets and then under the auspices of an "international debt regime." [Lipson (1981) argues that a system of unified private action, ad hoc conferences, emerged from the experiences of private lenders during the period when capital markets were essentially unregulated, and that IMF supervision is distinctive among international economic regimes, especially because of the reliance on nonstate actors as the primary source of rules, norms and procedures. The oil price shocks of 1970s, tight money policies of certain First World governments and other events then created a global recession that made it exceedingly difficult for Third World countries to meet their financial obligations.]

Although conventional wisdom says that the increased availability of financial resources and global recession alone account for indebted economic growth and that certain Third World governments failed to adjust to the latter event, it is a mistake to conclude that these factors explain this phenomenon (Brau, et al., 1983). The origins of indebted economic growth can also be traced to the character of political-economic relations within Third World countries, particularly the intervention of Third World states. In many countries, governments have actively promoted state and local-private enterprise as substitutes for foreign enterprise. This expansion of native enterprise has been financed in international capital markets, the state frequently providing loan guarantees to foreign lenders. The decline in the relative importance of direct foreign investment and the rise in indirect foreign investment thus has been, from the beginning, a consequence of the entrepreneurship of Third World states. In addition, governments' abilities to manage the distributional consequences of growth continue to be important determinants of foreign investment. Governments capable of resisting "social and political pressures" or demands for "excessive consumption" supposedly are more likely to repay their debts. Authorities who refuse to exercise such "political discipline" have been considered less likely to meet their financial obligations; the corresponding governments have had much more difficulty securing loans, regardless of their entrepreneurial proclivities (Bergsten, 1982:A27; *Numero: Revista De Economia Y Negocios,* 18 April 1982:11; *Business Latin America,* 3 June 1981:174; *Citibank Economic Letter,* January 1981). Analysis of the political economy of Third World countries —particularly the motivation for an consequence of the intervention of Third World states — is essential for understanding and evaluating the phenomenon of indebted economic growth.

A substantial body of theory on the political economy of Third World development exists, which can be used to make such a (revised) study of indebted economic growth. This monograph refines and applies major lines of argument within that literature. In chapter 2, the phenomenon is explained in terms of Hirschman's (1958) notion of the "functions" of growth. States' attempts to perform these functions lead them to make a series of policy choices that increase national output but also augment external financial obligations. The Latin American experience is shown to be rooted in just such a policy sequence.

Cross-national differences in patterns of indebted economic growth are analyzed in chapter 3 by expressing the argument in chapter 1 diagrammatically; specifically, constructing a model in which combinations of indebtedness and output result from states' (simultaneous) efforts to alter the income distribution and respond to demands for entrepreneurial assistance to and substitution for local entrepreneurs, under certain stylized conditions approximating the situation faced by Third World states in the late 1960s and the 1970s. The model is used to explain variations in the indebted economic growth of several Latin American countries. It also is used to study the policy options available to states given various growth targets and given (externally imposed) limits on indebtedness.

The results are applied, in chapter 4, in an extended discussion of the Brazilian experience. Brazilian authorities are shown to have believed that the state had to fulfill the (theoretically) expected functions if output was to increase; it examines how the series of policies they adopted could have produced the observed pattern of indebted economic growth. But questions arise about whether that policy sequence was *required* to augment national output. That is, the analysis suggests that it was not necessary for Brazilian authorities to have promoted income inequality as long as this policy was not a condition for securing foreign loans.

Chapter 5 briefly examines the experiences of several other Latin American countries and makes suggestions for further research on the phenomenon of indebted economic growth.

2

THIRD WORLD INDEBTEDNESS AND THE FUNCTIONS OF ECONOMIC DEVELOPMENT

Two basic tasks must be carried out in the course of economic development — the entrepreneurial and reform functions. The manner in which these two tasks are jointly performed within countries explains why there has been a shift to indirect foreign investment in many Third World countries and also why the phenomenon of indebted economic growth has come about. States have much to do with how the functions are carried out in that they promote entrepreneurship and manage the imbalances and inequities that inevitably surface in the course of economic development. Application of this theoretical framework reveals that differences in character and the extent of these forms of state intervention are the keys to understanding patterns of indebted economic growth.

In what follows, each function is described separately, and its relation to trends in foreign investment explained. A new account of indebted economic growth then is constructed by considering how the two functions are interrelated and carried out through a series of policy interventions that produce the phenomenon of indebted economic growth.

STATE ENTREPRENEURSHIP

The entrepreneurial function is the basis for capital accumulation. Its purpose is to promote existing industries, initiate new business ventures, and, more generally, provide the legal and institutional framework that makes possible the orderly operation of markets. Governments have long been involved in the performance of the entrepreneurial function; entrepreneurship is an important source of government revenue. The welfare of citizens depends, to a great degree, on whether (how) this entrepreneurial function is carried out. Indeed, "a state that ignores the necessity of assisting the process of capital accumulation risks drying up the source of its own power, the economy's surplus production capacity and the taxes drawn from this surplus (and other forms of capital) (O'Connor, 1973:6).

Of course, the scope and character of governmental assistance differs greatly across countries, ranging from entrepreneurial *support* to entrepreneurial *substitution* (Jones, 1975; Choski, 1979). Governments often provide the essential services required by private enterprise to carry out the entrepreneurial function: law and order, education and public health ("social overhead capital"), and infrastructural facilities such as transport, communications and electrical power (Hirschman, 1958). While entrepreneurial support usually entails the construction and operation of infrastructural facilities, the practice of providing and underwriting the financing for private entrepreneurship also is an important way in which public authorities assist the process of capital accumulation. Through loans and loan guarantees, governments provide essential services to entrepreneurs (Cameron, 1972).

These supports do not always effectively promote economic development, however; state support may not be an adequate stimulus to entrepreneurs. Private enterprise sometimes requires more than social overhead capital and/or financial guarantees, particularly in the advanced stages of industrialization when large sums of capital and sophisticated technology are needed if development is to continue. In such circumstances, governments often substitute as entrepreneur. Authorities create state enterprises that not only negotiate joint ventures with private enterprises but also expand (create) industries — industries that encourage capital accumulation. This is not to say that the state necessarily becomes an entrepreneur. Again, the state often serves as a substitute for private entrepreneurs: governments continue to take social considerations into account while at the same time emphasizing certain entrepreneurial objectives such as returns on (public) equity (for example, in deciding where to build and expand publicly owned plants, governments frequently take regional inequities into account). In this sense, entrepreneurial substitution is one factor responsible for the multiplicity of objectives that state-owned enterprises pursue (Choski, 1979: Sec. 2; Gillis, 1980:259-266). (The role of state enterprise in carrying out the reform function of development is mentioned below.)

The Third World experience differs from that of the First World in the character of the economic and political constraints on the entrepreneurship function, that is, the greater necessity for entrepreneurial support and substitution by the state in the former case (Freeman, 1982b). The native-private sector in many developing countries has been unwilling or unable to accomplish the entrepreneurial function. Especially in the advanced stages of industrialization, the various forms of governmental support simply would not ensure that native-private enterprise could continue to accumulate capital. This is not true for foreign enterprise, however. Foreign entrepreneurs have benefited greatly from the entrepreneurial support provided by Third World states, e.g., low-cost utility and transport facilities, but the outcome is that capital often has accumulated outside the national economy. Although foreign enterprise has generated tax revenues for the state, through such practices as the repatriation of profits, it has often exploited the productive capacity of Third World economies without necessarily strengthening them. Moreover, foreign enterprise has affected the viability of native entrepreneurship. Third World native-private industries cannot compete with the superior resources and technological sophistication of foreign firms; even if governments provide financial and other forms of entrepreneurial support, there is no guarantee that this function of economic growth will be carried out (Hirschman, 1958:202-205; 1971). Finally, government support for foreign enterprise has far-reaching political consequences. Owners of native-private firms desire the national accumulation of capital; yet, in many instances, they are themselves incapable of performing the entrepreneurial function, even with the support of their government. At the same time, these native entrepreneurs are influential members of society; political authorities cannot ignore their demands for protection and support of national interests.

Faced with opposition to state-supported, foreign entrepreneurship, Third World governments have had little choice but to greatly augment support for local enterprises and/or to substitute for foreign enterprise. Regardless of which strategy was adopted, it required the securing of adequate sums of capital and technology to ensure that the entrepreneurial function could be carried out. Once more, this problem was particularly severe in Third World countries, especially those on the threshold of advanced industrialization, for, in these cases, returns on the large sums of capital expended would not be immediately forthcoming. If these governments were to provide sound financing for the purpose of promoting national entrepreneurship, they would have to seek external sources of capital. Of course, government might print money for this purpose. In fact, it has been argued that the source of the Third World debt crisis lies in the manner in which governments such as Mexico manage their money supply (*Numero: Revista De Economia Y Negocios*, 18 April

11

1982:11).

It is at this point that the post-World War II internationalization of banking becomes relevant. It was this seemingly fortuitous event that gradually made the external financing of state entrepreneurship a *possibility*. Third World governments have been able to seek support for local business ventures by providing loan guarantees to foreign commercial banks. Where private enterprise has been less capable (or has been judged unfit) to perform the entrepreneurial function, governments have been able to seek external financing for publicly owned business ventures from those international lenders not opposed to state entrepreneurship. In the early 1950s, multilateral financial institutions often were unwilling to finance publicly owned business ventures (Bacha and Diaz-Alejandro, 1982:6).

In Latin America, governments' involvement in the entrepreneurial function led to the emergence of a "coalitional duo" between the state and foreign enterprise; this duo eventually gave way to a "tri-pe" or triple alliance between state, local and multinational capital (Collier, 1979:29). Since the early stages of Latin American economic development, states have assisted the process of capital accumulation. For example, while many of the first Latin American railroads were constructed by foreigners, native-private entrepreneurs also were active in railroad construction at the same time. States like Brazil had a hand in this activity; in the 1850s the government of Brazil took the initiative and provided the capital for the extension of a railroad into the coffee-rich Paraiba valley (Evans, 1976:35). Nor is indirect foreign investment a new phenomenon in Latin America. The Brazilian government floated its first bond in Europe in the 1820s (Frieden, 1981; Mc Knight, 1983).

Over time, Latin American governments became actively involved in infrastructural activities as well as other forms of entrepreneurial support such as domestic financing of local business ventures [Economic Commission for Latin America (ECLA), 1974]. While native enterprise benefited from these efforts, foreign firms, because of their relative size and technological sophistication, captured a greater and greater share of the productive capacity of Latin American economies, at the expense of native enterprise. In an attempt to arrest this trend, governments assumed a greater role in basic industries, either by becoming a major shareholder in mixed enterprise companies or by actually taking these kinds of entrepreneurial ventures on their own. For instance, the ECLA reported that the enlargement of the Brazilian state steel industry in the 1960s was due to the "lack of aggressive action by [local] private industry" (ECLA, 1964:160-61). In some countries, basic industries were nationalized due to expressly political considerations, e.g., the perceived need for "national champions" and/or conflict with particular multinational firms. Supposedly, the Mexican petroleum and Bolivian tin industries became state-owned firms for such reasons (ECLA, 1974:4).

Several countries found themselves in a situation where the entrepreneurial function was being performed largely — albeit not totally — by state and foreign enterprise. Native entrepreneurs reacted by demanding a greater role for national enterprise, and a strong stand against direct foreign investment became a requisite for the legitimation of governmental authority. For example, with regard to Mexican experience, Bennett and Sharpe (1980;180) wrote, "After World War II...nationalization became a very uncommon response of the Mexican government to foreign investment: 'Mexicanization' became the preferred strategy. In order to regulate and control the activities of transnational corporations and to protect and promote the growth of a Mexican national bourgoisie, foreign investors were first encouraged and then required to share majority ownership (equity) with Mexican partners... In these cases, the 'need' for state intervention arose not so much from the financial and technical requisites of the industrializing strategy as from the *political requisites* of the Mexicanization posture toward foreign investment" (emphasis mine). (On the importance of satisfying the demands of Brazilian native-private enterprise, see Evans, 1979:282-90).

In response, Latin American governments greatly increased their entrepreneurial support for native enterprise and, to differing degrees, expanded their state business sectors. In an attempt to incorporate native entrepreneurs into their development alliances, national financial institutions not only were given much greater authority to assist native-private firms, but states provided guarantees for borrowing international capital both for their own agencies and for native-private enterprises. In this way, governments such as Mexico moved beyond the realm of infrastructural and financial support to become the "bankers" of economic development (Bennett and Sharpe, 1980, 1982; Baer and Villela, 1980).

In addition, governments which, for the most part, controlled only basic industries, now began to acquire state firms in virtually all sectors of their economies so that state enterprises not only became quite numerous, but also contributed a substantial share of national output. The structures of the Brazilian and Mexican economies exemplify the entrepreneurial substitution that occurred in the Third World. By the early 1970s the Brazilian state owned about 56 percent of the assets in the largest fifty firms in its economy, while the Brazilian native-private sector accounted for only 16 percent of these assets (Newfarmer and Mueller, 1975). Over the same period, state-owned businesses have been a major force in Brazil's economy, contributing a comparatively high value added per worker and as much as 60 percent of Brazil's Gross Fixed Capital Formation (Mendonca de Barros and Graham, 1978; Trebat, 1983). In the early 1980s the state owned eighty-two of the largest 200 nonfinancial firms in Brazil, and these state enterprises accounted for almost 50 percent of the after-tax profit and employment of this collection of firms (*Visao,* 29 August 1981). Native-private enterprise plays a somewhat more important role in the Mexican economy. But, in this country as well, government owns and operates a core group of industries. In the early 1970s the shares of assets of the fifty largest Mexican business enterprises amounted to 38 percent and 42 percent for native-private and state enterprise, respectively (Newfarmer and Mueller, 1975). By the mid-1970s Mexican state undertakings generated almost 45 percent of that country's Gross Domestic Product. [See Whiting (1981) for information on the contribution of state enterprise to Mexican national output and a review of the larger role of the public sector in Mexico's economy.]

One important factor that contributed to governments' willingness to expand state enterprise was (is) the fact that, over time, entrepreneurial substitution enhanced the power and influence of an increasingly autonomous state sector bureaucracy, a bureaucracy that sometimes was both willing and able to expand state-owned firms against the wishes of incumbent political authorities. In fact, in some cases, the managers of state enterprises have bought up the holdings of foreign firms seemingly to further their own personal interests (Bennett and Sharpe, 1980:181; Collier, 1979:52). This has led to charges of "estatizacao" (statization). [See Evans, 1979:89-90, 282-90. Technobureaucratic legitimation is studied in Duvall and Freeman (1983); the interplay of local, state and multinational entrepreneurship is analyzed in greater detail in Freeman (1982a).] It also led to warnings about the effects of "autonomization." {In writing about the evolution of mixed character of Brazil's economy, Martins (1981) argues that as government businesses "come to count on stable revenues, administering and reproducing them in a quasi-entrepreneurial fashion, establishing their own salary structure, maintaining their own personnel recruitment procedures and social insurance system... [there inevitably arises] an 'esprit de corps' which creates a unique [institutional] personality. It is thus not surprising that these entities behave according to their own 'logic.' [Their] staff will identify with the enterprise's problems and goals rather than with those of the state. It is in this sense that [one can refer to]...the 'autonomization' of firms — the existence of a centrifugal trend within the state apparatus" (Bruneau and Faucher, 1981:79-80).}

As a consequence of the practice of entrepreneurial substitution, the *relative* magnitude of direct foreign investment has declined in some countries. But the outcome of state entrepreneurship has been essentially the same as that associated with earlier policies of entrepreneurial support — countries like Brazil and Mexico continue to rely on external sources of capital to promote economic development. This is because the financing for the recent creation and expansion of state-owned firms has been sought in international capital markets. In other words, the need to satisfy the political demands of native-private entrepreneurs and state enterprise managers has produced a willingness, on the part of Latin American governments, to sanction substantial increases in foreign indebtedness as a substitute for continued reliance on direct foreign investment. For example, Frieden (1981) reports that among developing countries public sector and publicly guaranteed loans account for between 80 and 90 percent of Eurocurrency credits. In the case of Mexico, in the last half of 1978, 83 percent of the external borrowing was of the public kind. Frieden's argument is that a substantial portion of these loans is motivated by state entrepreneurship. The demands for external sources of capital can be traced, in part, to the way states promote (carry out) the entrepreneurial function of economic development. (Morgan Guaranty Trust now provides data on Eurocurrency loan spreads on bank credits to governments and state enterprises. See *World Financial Markets,* August 1982:9.)

AUTHORITARIAN POLITICS

Sectoral imbalances and social inequities invariably surface in the course of economic development. These imbalances and inequities may impede development by creating supply bottlenecks on the one hand and civil unrest on the other. Economic growth, therefore, is the result of the successful performance of a second major task:

> At some point after the [entrepreneurial] function has had its run there will be efforts at catching up on the part of lagging sectors and regions, at social reforms to improve the welfare and position of groups that have been neglected or squeezed, and at redistribution of wealth and income in general. This is the "equilibrating," distributive or *reform* function (Hirschman, 1979:88).

In contrast to the entrepreneurial function, which is "pressure-producing," the reform function is "pressure-relieving" (Hirschman,

1958:202-205). If the reform function is carried out successfully, sectoral imbalances and social inequities will be ameliorated or the demands for redistribution will be effectively managed so that capital can continue to accumulate and output can expand still further.

There are a number of ways in which the performance of the reform function encouraged Third World indebtedness. For example, entrepreneurial assistance and substitution were often aimed at eliminating sectoral imbalances and redressing social inequities. Governments recognized the severe structural inadequacies of industrializing economies and provided entrepreneurial assistance to particular firms and/or undertook industrial ventures in underdeveloped sectors. In addition, governments sometimes used the employment, pricing and purchasing policies of state-owned firms to enhance the welfare of particular groups of citizens (Jones, 1981). The reform function, then, provided an impetus for government policies which, in turn, translated into greater demands for loans in international capital markets. However, this second function of growth is not merely another source of loan demand. The manner in which the reform function was carried out had consequences for the creditworthiness of Third World countries. The ability of governments to actually finance programs of entrepreneurial assistance and substitution depended, in part, on the extent to which loans were used to satisfy demands for income redistribution rather than for investment and, more generally, governments' abilities to manage distributional conflict.

In the First World the reform function has involved the gradual extension of citizenship rights (Marshall, 1950; O'Connor, 1973:162-68). For example, enfranchisement allowed more individuals to participate in collective decisions about social inequality and legitimized governmental authority in many Western countries (Freeman and Snidal, 1982). The extension of social rights went a step further by providing citizens with guarantees against certain inequities. According to many commentators, it was this latter component of citizenship — the entitlements that form the basis of the modern welfare state — that ensured the success of the reform function during the crisis of the 1930s. By disallowing certain inequities and providing safeguards against various forms of risk and uncertainty, advanced industrial societies have, so far, avoided social conflict over the distributional consequences of economic development (Offe, 1982; Prezworski and Wallerstein, 1982). [It is unclear whether the extension of social rights has had a deleterious impact on the entrepreneurial function over time, and hence diminished the likelihood of continued growth and social harmony in the First World (Bluestone and Harrison, 1982: chp.7; Katz, Mahler and Franz, 1983).]

Citizens of many Third World countries have, at one time or another, enjoyed some of the same rights and privileges that citizens in advanced industrialized countries enjoy. And Third World political institutions, including representative institutions, have been scenes of heated struggles over distributional issues. Today, however, most individuals in developing countries do not participate in decisions on the entrepreneurial or reform functions. Where citizens do possess suffrage, authorities often control the outcomes of elections by, for example, imposing restrictions on the ballot or by consistently reappointing incumbent politicians to representative institutions. Authorities also go to great lengths to manage the processes of interest articulation and interest aggregation. Unions and business associations often are directly incorporated into the government in order that demands for economic and social reform can be more easily managed. Consequently, individuals in most Third World countries simply do not enjoy the same entitlements or the same guarantees against economic risk and uncertainty as their First World counterparts, largely because the redistributive element of the reform function is believed to pose a threat to economic development.

Distributional equity is, according to the dominant view, a natural outgrowth of the development process: the dualistic nature of Third World economies is such that, in the intermediate stages of development, workers in the modern sector *must* earn substantially more than workers in the traditional sector, *and* the profit rates in the former *must* be higher than those in the latter. Wage and profit disparities are necessary to attract skilled labor and savings, both of which are in short supply. Since a viable modern sector *must* evolve before equal wage and profit rates can occur, toleration of income disparities at the intermediate stages of development is, in essence, a requisite for achieving a just pattern of economic development over the long term (Kuznets, 1979. See also the summaries in Frank and Webb, 1977: ch. 2, and Taylor, et al., 1980: ch. 10).

The extension of political rights supposedly reduces Third World societies' toleration of distributional inequities and hence prevents them from realizing their potential for economic development. The combination of suffrage and pluralistic forms of interest intermediation allows groups to press demands for income redistribution, which, in turn, forces governments to adopt policies that reduce wage disparities and discourage savings in the modern sector. The shortage of skilled labor becomes more acute and there is less saving and investment in the local economy. Governments have difficulty providing entrepreneurial assistance to private enterprises and in using state-owned firms to eliminate structural bottlenecks and promote growth, since they now must be concerned with distributional issues; for instance, their state-owned firms must provide certain groups of citizens with job security. Pluralistic politics thus supposedly produce gains in distributional equity but reductions in (aggregate) consumption in the long term. Authoritarian politics, on the other hand, can ignore (suppress) demands for resolving distributional equities.

Realization of Third World countries' long-term development potential is thought to be much easier under authoritarian rule (see the summary in Frank and Webb, 1977:15-19). Apparently, this view is held by heads of most multinational corporations and international lending institutions as well as by many Third World business people and political authorities. Multinational and local firms alike prefer stable, risk-free investment climates that promote high rates of return on investments (Frank, 1980:26-27). International lenders are primarily interested in countries' ability to service (and sometimes repay) their debts out of future export earnings and increases in national output. [The problems of capital flight pose severe difficulties for governments that pursue redistributive policies (Girvan, 1980; Balassa, 1977). Balassa even suggests that luxury taxes may be the best way to redistribute income while minimizing the effect on local investment.] Finally, political authorities and heads of some multinational lending institutions, besides having a personal stake in gaining (maintaining) their power and wealth, often consider themselves guardians of the interests of future generations. Authoritarianism, in their eyes, enhances the welfare of unborn citizens. The extension of political rights therefore is opposed by a wide range of groups who see their individual interests and, to some extent, (Third World) societies' collective interests best served by an authoritarian kind of politics where it is up to a small group of elites to decide whether certain inequities are to be tolerated or not.

The scope of the political restrictions on citizenship, combined with the effects of social inequities themselves, enables Third World governments to resist demands for reform and remain in authority. Controls on elections and other forms of political expression allow ruling elites to manage the debates over the distributional consequences of development. For instance, corporatist forms of interest intermediation facilitate control over the content of the demands articulated in representative institutions. In addition, deliberate refusal to redress social inequality serves to forestall the development of mass politics. In fact, Sheahan (1980:272) and others have gone so far as to argue that, with regard to mass politics, "conditions of extreme poverty and ignorance for major parts of a country's population keeps citizens politically inert, as thoroughly excluded from participation in social decisions as if they were subject to direct (political) repression." [At the local level, however, there is evidence of interest articulation and aggregation, even among the poorest groups of citizens (Cornelius, 1975).] In rejecting calls for reform, authorities also gain support from native and foreign business people, who not only receive a greater share of a countries' scarce resources but also, above all, consider their investments more profitable and secure over the long term (Evans, 1979: ch. 6). Last, and most important for our purposes, until recently, authoritarian politics assured international lenders of governments' abilities to service and repay their debts. For international lenders, authoritarian politics generally meant that the development process was much more likely to take its natural course, that profits would accumulate from new investments and that these profits would be used to meet borrowers' external financial obligations, rather than to redress social inequities. Moreover, as more loans were made in the 1960s and 1970s, more resources became available for entrepreneurial assistance and substitution. And more entrepreneurial assistance and substitution generally produced still more support from some key groups within Third World societies, even though, as noted earlier, state entrepreneurship created problems for governments over time. In this way, the buildup of foreign debts, for a time, imparted legitimacy to authoritarian governments and made possible still further (foreign) loans on the grounds that they were able to manage the reform function in a way that would not jeopardize their country's long-term growth potential.

In most Latin American countries, the reform function has been carried out "from above" by regimes of an "organic-statist" variety (Hirschman, 1979:96-97; Stepan, 1978). Working within a concession theory of interest groups that allows for limited pluralism, Latin American governments have created political and economic institutions that will allow them to shape the scope and content of debates over the distributional consequences of development. Earlier in this century, this entailed the extension of political rights and concerted efforts to ameliorate social inequality. In the 1960s and 1970s, though, citizenship rights often were retracted and distributional inequities were ignored or even promoted by political authorities.

This change in Latin American government policies can be traced to the installation of authoritarian regimes that ascribed to the belief that short-term inequities were a prerequisite of economic development, and to the support these regimes received from international lenders who shared that view. In Brazil, for example, a military coup and a series of government decrees produced an authoritarian government that actively suppressed political participation and sanctioned social inequities.

Brazilian Finance Minister Simonsen (1971-1979) explained the rationale for this:

> Organizing the aspirations of society into a feasible program of action is the great challenge to government officials of the modern world, and it is unfortunately necessary to admit that many of them have been unable to accomplish this task. It is also unfortunate but true that universal suffrage frequently rewards those candidates who promise to divide resources into parts whose sum is greater than the whole. This leads to an excessive emphasis on "disruptive" policies whose consequences include rapid inflation, external indebtedness, the failure of growth, and social disorder (Simonsen, 1974a:2).

In other words, Brazilians' political freedoms had to be restricted in order that conflict over social inequities not threaten the entrepreneurial function of growth. Social inequities had to be tolerated (and in some cases actually promoted, with expressed political designs). Since income transfers or other means of redistribution would serve "probably to increase the demand for food, but diminish the demand for automobiles, the result of a sudden redistribution would be merely to generate inflation in the food-producing sector and excess capacity in the car industry" (Simonsen, 1974b:66). Another illustration of this logic appears in the foreword to Carlos Langoni's study of Brazilian income inequality, written by the well-known Brazilian Minister Antonio Delfim Netto. He states:

> Langoni *proves* that the observed increase in inequality is a direct consequence of market disequilibria accompanying the development process. Thus, the behavior of relative incomes reflects, mostly, the intense process of differentiation of the labor force caused by the rapid expansion of modern sectors. In these sectors, however, workers are very productive and, because of this, receive relatively high earnings even when the variance is larger. In this context, it makes no sense to use the increased in inequality as an index of welfare deterioration (Delfim Netto, 1973:14).

McDonough (1980, 1981) found additional evidence of the belief in the necessity of authoritarian politics and income inequality in his interviews with Brazilian elites. Hamiliton (1975:103) argues that the same set of beliefs motivated many of the policies of the Alemon government that ruled Mexico in the 1940s.

There is much debate (reviewed below) about whether income inequality is a natural outgrowth of the development process and, either way, whether authoritarian politics is the most effective way to manage the demands for ameliorating these inequities. Some Third World countries have achieved rapid growth while income redistribution was being promoted (Ahn, 1983). There is little empirical basis for some of the claims on which the inherent inequality thesis rests (Frank and Webb, 1977:n. 7 to ch. 2), and data analyses yield somewhat *inconsistent* results as to whether democracy promotes income equality in the Third World (Weede and Tiefenbach, 1981) and whether democracy retards economic development (Marsh, 1979). Yet, Simonsen's and other Latin American policy maker's views apparently were shared by most members of the international financial community. By all indications, international lenders were convinced that political liberalization and/or the extension of social entitlements threatened to retard economic development and that reforms would make it more difficult for Latin American countries to meet their financial obligations. They therefore supported the installation of authoritarian regimes — and especially the disciplining of labor — in Latin America, and greatly increased the amount of capital they were willing to loan there (See Freeman, 1983). As foreign debts began to accumulate, lenders continually expressed their confidence in Latin American governments' willingness and ability to implement the "domestic adjustments" necessary to service their foreign debts.

In sum, the manner in which the reform function has been carried out by Latin American and other Third World governments has enabled them to *secure* external sources of capital for performing the entrepreneurship function. These governments would have been considered much less creditworthy had they been managing the reform function within a pluralistic political framework. Authoritarian politics and a (mutual) belief in the need to tolerate social inequities ensured credit-worthiness. And just such a style of rule and set of elite dispositions prevailed in many Third World countries in the 1960s and 1970s.

REEXAMINING THE ORIGINS OF INDEBTED ECONOMIC GROWTH

The shifting character of Third World dependence — the increasing importance of *indirect* foreign investment — is in part an outcome of the sequential unfolding of the two functions of economic development, or series of governmental policies that were both consequences of and motivations for state intervention of an entrepreneurial-authoritarian kind. Governments' early involvement in the entrepreneurial function encouraged direct foreign investment at the expense of native entrepreneurship. Limited economic growth was achieved, but that growth was accompanied by demands for the reform of social inequality and for the promotion of national enterprise. Governments responded by offering greater assistance to the entrepreneurial function and, in some cases, by extending political rights and social rights. But, in the process, many Third World countries had difficulty developing further; in particular, they were unable to generate adequate amounts of domestic and/or foreign capital to meet the needs of native entrepreneurs while simultaneously answering calls for greater social equality.

In some countries, state entrepreneurship was accompanied by a gradual retraction of political freedoms and the sanctioning of social inequities. In other cases, conflict over the distribution of wealth produced major crises out of which emerged regimes willing and able both to promote state enterprise and to rescind many of its citizens' rights (Hirschman, 1979). That these regimes' entrepreneurial proclivities produced demands for external sources of capital is widely recognized. What is not adequately appreciated is how Third World governments' approach to managing the reform function enhanced their credit-worthiness and thus made it possible for them to actually *secure* the financing for entrepreneurial assistance and substitution. Third World borrowers' abilities to service their debts would have been more closely scrutinized and many more "political strings" would have been attached to the loans they received, if, in the respective countries, the reform function had been managed through a pluralistic form of politics, especially if pluralism had resulted in a greater emphasis on consumption than on investment and income transfers from the rich to the poor.

The failure to appreciate the importance of the reform dimension is evident in the works of Frieden, and Bacha and Diaz-Alejandro, for example. Frieden studied trends in indirect foreign investment in the Third World and concluded that the shift from direct foreign investment has occurred primarily because of the entrepreneurial proclivities of governments, especially authorities' willingness to substitute as entrepreneur. Frieden claims that "these nationalistic state-capitalist regimes have joined with the internationalist finance-capitalists of the Euromarkets: the banks provide the capital, the state provides the muscle and brains to force-march countries into the industrialized world" (1981:408). However, Frieden never considers the role of the reform dimension (the importance of regimes' willingness to *"force-march"* their countries into the advanced stages of industrialization). Rather, he emphasizes the current availability of finance capital and the willingness of Third World countries to borrow without fully explaining how it is that restrictions on citizenship are necessary to actually secure these loans (e.g., see his summary of the "beauty" of the Mexican arrangement).

Bacha and Diaz-Alejandro argue that "on balance, semi-industrialized countries were helped during the 1970s by the emergence and expansion of private international financial markets. True enough, private credits were more costly and shorter-term than official bilateral or multilateral finance. However, volumes were larger, procedures were more expeditious, and looser strings were attached, both at the political and at the economic-policy levels.'' They go on to note that "the opportunities created by the new international capital markets may not generate welfare gains in every borrowing country. Funds may be raised cheaply but spent so foolishly as to create repayment problems, and the availability of external finance can lead to lower domestic savings. By changing the nature of external economic incentives and penalties, the fluid international financial market nudged Latin American and other LDC economies into a new mold during the 1970s. In principle, it extended the range of options opened to economic policy-making, providing new opportunities for economic gain. But it also shaped the system of economic incentives in particular directions and induced some shifts of relative economic power within countries. In this context, the rules of access established by domestic policy-makers seem to have been a basic determinant of the short- to medium-term economic and social consequences of financial openness'' (1982:28).

Thus these authors imply that foreign borrowing and "financial openness" provide opportunities for augmenting the level of societal wealth and (implicitly) the distribution of wealth, without considering the possibility that there were political conditions under which borrowing and openness were accomplished and that these conditions precluded certain welfare outcomes from being realized.

Indebted economic growth is, in large part, the result of borrowers' and lenders' failure to realize the ineffectiveness of the state entrepreneurial-authoritarian development strategy or that the sequence of policies adopted by Third World governments serve more to create unrealistic expectations among public authorities and their creditors than to promote self-sustaining growth. It is true that output expanded in many of the countries that adopted the state entrepreneurial-authoritarian strategy and that foreign-financed state enterprises accounted for a substantial share of the increase in output. But it is unclear whether foreign-financed policies of entrepreneurial assistance were responsible for the *rate* of growth that these countries enjoyed, particularly in the late 1960s and the 1970s. It can be argued that these growth rates were instead the result of a cyclical upturn in the global economy. Also, there is much evidence in general that state-owned firms simply aren't as productive as privately owned firms and that this is true even if they are unfettered by interest group demands. For example, managers apply different efficiency criteria in operating publicly owned firms and in many countries they lack the experties of their counterparts in the private sector (Gillis, 1980). Over time, then, entrepreneurial substitution may have the effect of slowing the rate of growth and hence, all things being equal, retarding countries' abilities to service foreign debts.

Similarly, there is little doubt that social inequities were tolerated in many indebted countries, and the authoritarian character of the corresponding governments clearly made it easier for them to repress (ignore) demands for redistribution and consumption and to promote saving and investment. And, as Bacha and Diaz-Alejandro (1982) point out, contrary to popular belief, many of the foreign loans secured in the 1960s and 1970s were used for investment rather than for consumption. However, as noted earlier, there is good reason to believe that social inequality could have been ameliorated and output might have expanded at the same rate.

The key to understanding the phenomenon of indebted economic growth is recognizing that many Third World elites and heads of international financial institutions *believed* in the efficacy of the state entrepreneurial-authoritarian development strategy. These beliefs caused them to consummate more and more loan agreements — agreements which, for a time, contributed to still further borrowing in that they temporarily legitimized governments, making public authorities appear even more able to achieve, through continued policies of entrepreneurial assistance and substitution and authoritarian management of the reform function, self-sustaining economic development. The misjudgments of the elites and their creditors were vividly illuminated when, in the 1970s, oil crises produced a global recession. But it is likely that indebted economic growth would have been prevalent in the late 1970s, even if the second oil shock had not been felt; the phenomenon is as much an outgrowth of over-optimistic beliefs in the effectiveness of the state entrepreneurial-authoritarian development strategy as it is the result of a failure to anticipate (cope with) events like the oil crisis. For instance, one can argue that commercial banks simply were securing outlets for the massive deposits they received from oil producers and/or that the growth rate of indebted Third World countries slowed because of the tight money policies Northern governments adopted in the aftermath of the second oil shock. Both arguments are relevant. But the first overlooks the fact that when banks discovered certain countries were unable to repay their debts they quickly constructed (entered into) a set of institutional arrangements which preserved the authoritarian character of the governments involved and promoted greater toleration of social inequities — albeit initially with less state entrepreneurship — with in the debtor countries (cf. Lipson, 1981; Stallings, 1979; Girvan, 1980). The substantial increase in the relative magnitude of debt to GDP and to GNP *prior to* 1978 is ignored by the second argument.

In the Latin American experience, the early formation of the coalition of state and foreign capital had much to do with the fact that in many countries citizens once enjoyed some political and social rights. In the period after World War II, state-assisted (direct) foreign investment weakened native entrepreneurship while the corporatist policies of some political parties allowed advocates of reform to capture or at least participate in collective decision making about social inequality. In turn, preferential treatment of native-private business was encouraged and various political rights and social entitlements were extended to Latin American citizens. This did not necessarily mean that ruling elites were replaced or that social inequalities were always eliminated. However, in the 1950s and 1960s governments did find it increasingly difficult to promote domestic capital accumulation *and* social equity. For example, in writing about the Latin American corporatism of the 1950s and 1960s, Malloy (1977:15) states that "the period saw a kind of de facto politics of informal and nonstructured inclusion which expanded the participants in the political game without any significant restructuring of that game." The failure to reach an acceptable compromise on state intermediation in the entrepreneurial and reform functions of development rendered some countries less credit-worthy in the eyes of the international financial community of that period. Hence foreign loans were more difficult to secure and governments' ability to maintain social harmony became even more tenuous.

Out of the ensuing crises emerged authoritarian regimes that were expressly capitalist in their orientation and quite opportunistic in their dealings in international economy:

> (these) authoritarian regimes try to accommodate themselves within the international environment by taking advantage of occasional fissures in the world's economic system. They make deals with multi-national enterprises that in some cases involve renegotiating the terms of dependency within narrow limits — though, in some cases, as in Chile, they do simply accept local and eventually international private interests as if they corresponded to the needs of the nation and of the people. Yet, as a rule, at the ideological and sometimes the practical level, they try to reinforce not the nation but the state — if not for other motives, then at least to protect their own interests as a bureaucracy (Cardoso, 1979:52-53).

It is these entrepreneurial-authoritarian states that in Latin America exploited the opportunity ("fissure") for indebted economic growth, ensuring their credit-worthiness by the way they managed the reform function and seeking legitimacy through the growth which their entrepreneurial support and substitution supposedly achieved.

The fact that they have become the major debtors in the world testifies to the fact that international lenders shared their beliefs in the efficacy of the state entrepreneurial-authoritarian development strategy. The fact that the Latin American experience exemplifies the phenomenon of indebted economic growth suggests that in this region more than any other, these beliefs were unjustified. To understand this, we must look more deeply into how policies of entrepreneurial assistance and substitution and the toleration of social inequities together produce a pattern of indebted economic growth. It is to this task that we now turn.

3

PATTERNS OF INDEBTED ECONOMIC GROWTH

Study of the sequential unfolding of the entrepreneurial and reform functions cast new light on the origins of indebted economic growth, particularly the role that state intervention played in encouraging the shift from reliance on direct foreign investment to reliance on indirect foreign investment. By focusing on certain, interrelated features of the policy-making process described in chapter 2, insights also can be gained into why individual countries experienced this shift in dependence when they did, as well as why states underwent particular series of transformations before ultimately assuming entrepreneurial-authoritarian forms. Among the factors to be considered in constructing such explanation of regime change are the ideological support for the two functions of economic growth within particular countries, the timing of different events (length of time before the state responds to the demands of native entrepreneurs), the configurations of power within different political economies and contextual variables such as the national endowments of Third World countries (Collier, 1979).

But this explanation does not tell us why particular histories of indebted economic growth are observed, or how the series of policies of different governments adopted are responsible for alternative patterns of indebted economic growth. Consider, for example, the short histories of Public Debt and Gross Domestic Product in figure 1. [Recall that Public Debt represents the major share of indebtedness recently incurred by countries like Mexico and Brazil. The following analysis focuses on causes and consequences of policy choice within developing countries. Hence these questions are posed in terms of debt to GDP ratios.]

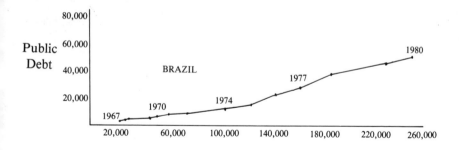

Gross Domestic Product
Indebted Economic Growth, Brazil

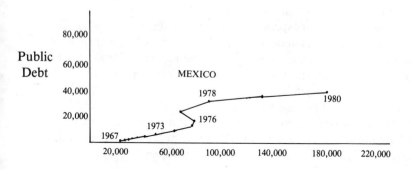

Gross Domestic Product
Indebted Economic Growth, Mexico

Figure. 1   Indebted Economic Growth of Selected Latin American
Countries.

28

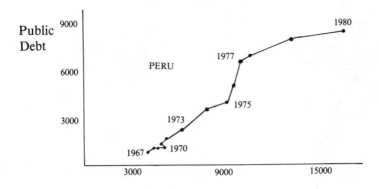

Gross Domestic Product
Indebted Economic Growth, Peru

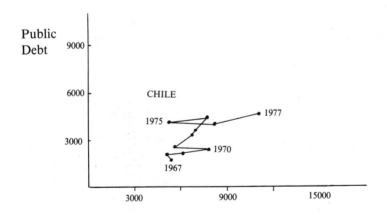

Gross Domestic Product
Indebted Economic Growth, Chile

Figure 1. (Cont.)

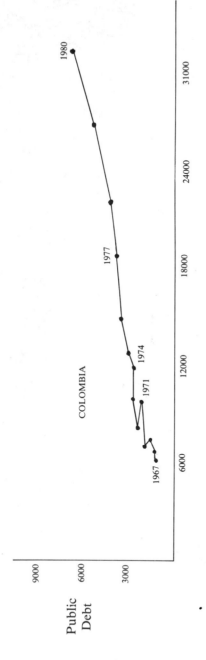

Gross Domestic Product Indebted Economic Growth, Colombia

Figure 1 (cont.)

Notes. Public debt is public and publicly guaranteed debt outstanding, including undisbursed, -- all lenders; figures in millions of U.S. dollars, current prices; source: *World Debt Tables External Public Debt* (December 31, 1982 and selected years). Gross Domestic Product is expressed in millions of U.S. dollars, current prices; source: *Yearbook of National Account Statistics*, volume II, 1979 and, for the years 1979 and 1980, *International Financial Statistics* 35(8), August 1982 [Implicit Market Rate/Market Rate conversion (rf) was used in this case.].

30

Data in figure 1 suggest that both Brazil and Peru experienced a similar, smooth rise in the ratio of public debt to GDP. But, in the Peruvian case, public debt represents a much larger share of national output. In what way are the policies of the Peruvian regime responsible for this outcome? What is it about the Peruvian economy that translates entrepreneurial assistance (substitution) and income (re)maldistribution into relatively higher ratios of debt to output? Also, the character of the political alliance that ruled Brazil in the 1970s was somewhat different from that which ruled Colombia. Yet, with the exception of a temporary reversal in 1972, the pattern of indebted economic growth is (qualitatively) similar in these two countries. Is this because the respective regimes carried out the entrepreneurial and reform functions in the same ways? Finally, how do we account for the chaotic nature of the Chilean case? Was the (partial) dismantling of Chile's state enterprise sector alone responsible for this pattern? If so, how is it that major reversals in (commitments to) state entrepreneurship and income (re)maldistribution produce such an unusual history of indebted economic growth?

The key to answering these questions lies in the process through which governments *simultaneously* managed the entrepreneurial and reform functions of economic development. To understand the similarities and differences suggested by figure 1, we must examine the motivations for and consequences of the policy mixes of these countries. I propose a diagrammatic framework that explains indebted economic growth in terms of how governments respond to demands for entrepreneurial assistance and substitution and how governments alter the (aggregate) demand for goods and services through income transfers. The framework is based on the idea that a set of indebted-output combinations is associated with each kind of policy intervention. That is, once government decides to provide entrepreneurial assistance and substitution, a set of indebtedness-output combinations obtain under which the demands for such intermediation are perfectly satisfied; similarly, once government decides to transfer wealth between income classes, (another) set of indebtedness-output combinations obtain under which the local demand for goods and services are satisfied. A particular mix of such policies then produces a (single) combination of indebtedness and output which corresponds to the joint equilibria in which both the demands for assistance and substitution *and* the demands for goods and services are satisfied. These joint equilibria obtain because of certain stylized assumptions about the way Third World markets and international lenders behave. Study of how these joint equilibria change under alternative kinds of policies explains the patterns in figure 1. The analysis also yields insights into the policy options available to governments that have certain growth targets and/or are constrained in the level of indebtedness they can (are willing to) incur.

The attempt to develop a formal framework with which to analyze Third World indebtedness is not new. For instance, Feder (1982) recently proposed a modified "growth-cum-indebtedness" formalism which incorporates the consequences of trade gaps for external borrowing. However, like most models in this genre (see Wallerstein, 1982), Feder's formulations do not allow for conflict over the distributional consequences of growth, either in terms of changing growth targets or alternative consumption profiles. The framework proposed here is in the spirit of a more general formulation of the policial economy of industrializing countries proposed some years ago by Przeworski and Cortes (1971), who investigated the problem of simultaneously regulating a party (electoral) system and an economic (distributive) system. They also explored various state strategies in this regard, with emphasis on explaining the Eastern European and Latin American experiences.

The diagrammatic framework departs in certain ways from various structuralist models of Third World economies. The implications of these departures are discussed in chapter 5, where several suggestions are made for recasting the model in a different form.

The discussion parallels the presentation in chapter 2. First, the effects of each type of policy choice are studied in isolation. Next, the consequences of adopting alternative mixes of state entrepreneurship and income redistribution are analyzed. On the basis of this investigation of (joint) indebtedness-output equilibria, some of the questions about Latin American patterns of indebted economic growth then are answered. A discussion of the policy options available to Third World governments concludes this section.

A FRAMEWORK FOR THE ANALYSIS OF INDEBTED ECONOMIC GROWTH

State entrepreneurship is motivated by a number of concerns, most notably, the demand for protection of national interests. Owners of native firms expect governments to promote domestic capital accumulation through entrepreneurial support and/or entrepreneurial substitution. How much state assistance is needed depends, in large part, on current levels of national output and indebtedness. The greater the national output of national entrepreneurs, the less need for entrepreneurial assistance from the state; as native firms accumulate capital through increased output, they have less difficulty securing foreign financing, and the need for loan

32

guarantees lessens. Native firms may even be able to rely on self-financing to some degree. In contrast, a decline in national output means diminished domestic capital accumulation and a greater need for state assistance; native entrepreneurship becomes less profitable and foreign capital is more difficult to secure.

Indebtedness also shapes the demands of native firms. High levels of indebtedness mean that native entrepreneurs have correspondingly high obligations to international creditors, and may indicate that domestic sources of credit are limited. As indebtedness increases, the state is asked to help (re)negotiate debt payments in order to maintain profitability and credit-worthiness. As indebtedness falls, on the other hand, demands for entrepreneurial assistance diminish, since the credit-worthiness of national enterprise is not in question.

Finally, there is a need for entrepreneurial assistance that is essentially unaffected by levels of output and indebtedness. This autonomous source of demand corresponds to the most basic of those needs previously referred to as "social overhead capital."

The various components of the demands for entrepreneurial assistance can be combined in the following way. Let the aggregate demands of native enterprise be denoted by DE and define $\overline{DE}$ as the autonomous component thereof. [I do not attempt to operationalize DE here. But, for the purposes of exposition, one could interpret the demand for entrepreneurial assistance as a (weighted) sum of all public guaranteed borrowing and the value of capital formation attributable to entrepreneurial support/substitution.] Then, with I and Y representing indebtedness and output, respectively, the demands which motivate state entrepreneurial assistance are:

$$DE = \overline{DE} + nY + kI, \tag{1}$$

where, in keeping with the argument above, we have $\overline{DE} > 0$: national enterprise always demands some assistance from public authorities; $n < 0$: there is an inverse relationship between national output and demand for entrepreneurial assistance or $\frac{\partial DE}{\partial Y} = n < 0$; and $k > 0$: indebtedness augments the demands for entrepreneurial assistance at the rate k, $\frac{\partial DE}{\partial I} = k > 0$.

Now, suppose a government decides to fix the level of entrepreneurial assistance at some SE'. (We consider the full range of options open to governments, below. Here we are concerned with explicating the basic political-economic relations underlying entrepreneurial assistance.) What are the ramifications of such a policy decision? Note that if state entrepreneurial assistance is set at some SE′ and that level of assistance exactly satisfies the demands for assistance, equation (1) can be rewritten:

$$SE' = DE = \overline{DE} + nY + kI,$$

from which it follows that, in equilibrium,

$$I = \tfrac{1}{k}(SE' - \overline{DE} - nY). \tag{2}$$

The implication of (2) is that there are alternative combinations of indebtedness and output under which SE′ would (exactly) satisfy the demands for assistance from native entrepreneurs; provision of and demand for entrepreneurial assistance could be in equilibrium under a variety of indebtedness and output conditions.

The collection of equilibria that could obtain under the policy of fixing state entrepreneurial assistance at SE′ is depicted in figure 2. Note, for instance, that as ξ_1 we have indebtedness of I_1 and output of Y_1, which result in demands equal to $DE_1 = SE'$.

At ξ_1, equation (1) becomes

$$DE_1 = \overline{DE} + nY_1 + kI_1,$$

so if native entrepreneurs' demands for assistance are met ($SE' = DE_1$), we have

$$I_1 = (\tfrac{1}{k})[SE' - \overline{DE} - nY_1]$$

At ξ_2, indebtedness is higher ($I_2 > I_1$), so more demands for assistance are forthcoming. Hence if the respective (aggregate) level of national enterprise's demands, DE_2, also is equal to SE′, output must be at the comparatively greater level of Y_2 (offsetting the increased demands for assistance that result from the higher level of indebtedness, I_2). By adjoining all such equilibrium pairs of indebtedness and output, we generate the *state entrepreneurship line* or, *SE line,* along which the SE′ policy exactly meets the demands for support and substitution from national enterprise.

To reiterate, along the state entrepreneurship line in figure 2 are the pairs of indebtedness and output that exactly satisfy nationalists' demands under the (fixed) policy SE′. The SE line has positive slope since if the equilibrium is at ξ_1 and indebtedness shifts to I_2, more assistance will be demanded and SE′ will continue to satisfy native enterprises' demands

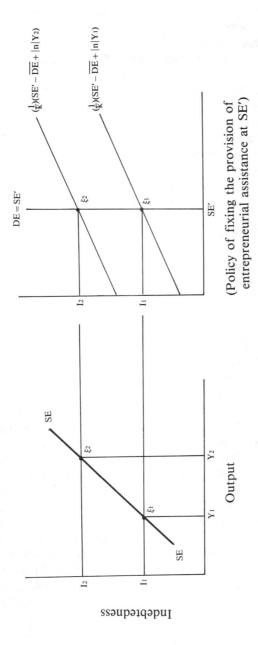

Figure 2. The SE Line Under the Policy of Fixing Entrepreneurial Assistance at SE'.

35

only if Y_1 also increases to some Y_2 thereby ensuring that the *net* change in these demands is zero.

Note that the focus is on demands for a certain amount of publicly guaranteed borrowing, public investment and so on, rather than on investment demand per se. [In most structuralist models, the South has no (endogenous) investment demand; Southern investment is essentially determined in the North (Taylor, 1981). The present model does share with neo-Keynesian models of Third World economies, the notion that investment is not determined by the amount of domestic saving but rather by nonmarket — here political — considerations (cf. Taylor, et al., 1980:7). As pointed out below, the phenomenon of "forced saving" is not explicitly incorporated into the model.]

Three properties of the state entrepreneurship line will be used in the subsequent analysis of governmental policy making. First, the relative impacts of indebtedness and output on the demands of national enterprise, DE, determine the equilibrium relation between these two factors, or, formally, the relation between $|n|$ and k determines the slope of the SE line. Rewriting equation (2) as

$$I = \tfrac{1}{k}[SE' - \overline{DE}] - \tfrac{|n|}{k}\, Y, \qquad (3)$$

we see that under a policy which fixes entrepreneurial assistance and substitution at SE', (SE' $-\overline{DE}$) is constant so the equilibrium relation between Y and I depends on the quotient $\tfrac{|n|}{k}$. This means that the greater the impact of output relative to the impact of indebtedness on DE ($|n| > k$), the smaller the increase in Y needed to offset the effects of higher indebtedness on demands for more state entrepreneurship. *If $|n|$ is much larger than k ($|n| > > k$), the SE line will be quite steep.* That is, a small increase in output causes a comparatively large reduction in the demand for state entrepreneurship so that a relatively great increase in I and, concomitantly, augmentation of demands for assistance in meeting external financial obligations would have to occur if SE' were to continue to exactly satisfy the (overall) demands of native firms. On the other hand, when the relative impact of indebtedness far exceeds that of output, ($k > > |n|$), a small increase in I translates into a large augmentation of DE and equilibrium is achieved only if output substantially increases, thereby allowing for a compensatory reduction in the (overall) demands for entrepreneurial assistance. *In this latter case ($k > > |n|$), then, the state entrepreneurship line is almost horizontal.*

A second important property of the state entrepreneurship line has to do with the effects of governments altering the level at which they fix policy: *a shift from SE' to a greater, fixed level of entrepreneurial assistance and substitution, SE''', moves the SE line to the southeast.* Suppose that the policy shifts from SE' to SE'' where SE'' > SE' and that indebtedness remains constant at I_1 (figure 3). Then, if this new policy, SE'', is in equilibrium — the demands of native entrepreneurs still are exactly met — output must decline to Y_1' and the excess supply of support and substitution (SE'' – SE') is provided as a result of the economic slowdown ($Y_1' – Y_1$). In other words, given indebtedness of I_1, there is an equilibrium, ξ_1' under the policy SE'', only if governments' readiness to promote native enterprise (SE'' – SE') is absorbed by increased demands for state entrepreneurship ensuing from a decline in output from Y_1 to Y_1'. Similar reasoning, for different combinations of indebtedness and output and the alternative direction of policy change, yields this second property of the SE line.

A third important feature of the model concerns the consequences of departures from equilibrium, i.e., the interpretation of indebtedness-output combinations that lie off the state entrepreneurship line. Consider the situation at E_1: (I_1, Y_2) in figure 4. At this point, which is *below the SE line, there is excess support and substitution being provided by the government.* At such a comparatively low level of indebtedness, and high level of output, the demand for entrepreneurial support and substitution is at some $DE_1 = SE_1 < SE'$; less state entrepreneurship would satisfy national enterprise's demands. In contrast, *at points above the SE line* such as E_2, *there is an excess demand for entrepreneurial assistance and substitution.* At E_2 the relatively high indebtedness and low output means that national enterprise is requesting more entrepreneurial support and substitution than the government is prepared to offer ($DE_2 = SE_2 > SE'$). Government is not satisfying the demands of native firms when the indebtedness-output combination is above the SE line.

In sum, demands for entrepreneurial support and substitution may vary with indebtedness and output while also depending on the more autonomous needs of native enterprise. Under the policy of fixing state entrepreneurship at some SE', the equilibrium conditions in indebtedness and output — the pairs (I, Y) that represent balance in the provision of and demand for entrepreneurial support and substitution — can be represented as the positively sloped SE line in figure 2. The steepness of this line depends on the relative impacts of indebtedness and output on the needs of native entrepreneurs; fixing state entrepreneurship at comparatively higher levels, SE'' > SE', shifts the equilibrium pairs of indebtedness and output, SE line, to the northwest, while reducing state entrepreneurship to some SE''' < SE' moves the SE line to the southeast;

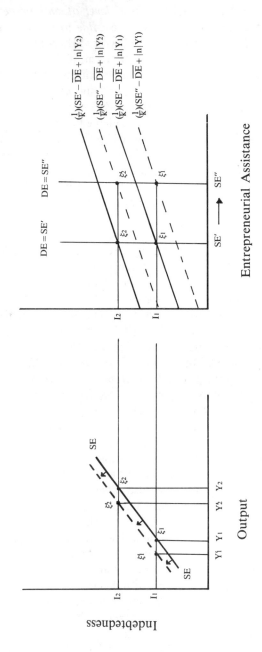

Figure 3. The Shift to a Greater, Fixed Level of Entrepreneurial Assistance at SE"

38

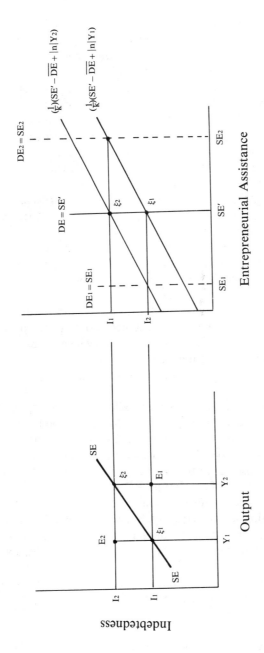

Figure 4. Combinations of Indebtedness and Output Which Lie off the SE Line

39

and, for the policy SE', combinations of I and Y below the SE line imply an excess of state entrepreneurship relative to the demands of national enterprise while combinations of indebtedness and output above the SE line connote an excess demand for state entrepreneurship.

Our study of the reform function implies that, in regard to the supposed tradeoff between economic inequality and domestic capital accumulation, Third World policy makers have a marked preference for domestic capital accumulation. Political authorities expressly sanction social and economic inequalities for the sake of economic growth. In terms of policy, this means that regimes seek to create a certain "consumption profile," or they promote "uneven expansion of consumption, uneven with respect to both kinds of articles and categories of consumers" (Hirschman, 1979:80-81). (Hirschman describes this *consequence* of Third World authoritarian regimes. However, he points out that the desire to implement such a strategy may have motivated certain groups to install authoritarian governments in Latin America.) This uneven expansion of consumption provides motivation for state intervention; wage policy and income transfers are managed to encourage the purchase of consumer goods by the wealthy, for instance.

Indebtedness may itself serve as a source of demand for domestically produced goods and services. For instance, external borrowing *may* stimulate purchases of products manufactured by local firms. Similarly, foreign financing of some national enterprises *may* augment the demand for various services provided by other native companies (e.g., shipping and transport).

The reform dimension of state intermediation can be represented in the following way: denote the aggregate demand for goods and services by DG and let $\overline{DG}$ represent the autonomous component of demand by consumers, investors and government. In the present formulation, $\overline{DG}$ is assumed to be insensitive to changes in indebtedness but indirectly affected by income transfers. Define EQ as the amount of resources transferred from upper to lower income groups for the expressed purpose of ameliorating social inequality. Suppose the effect of an increase in EQ is to render the income distribution more equitable but, conceivably, to diminish total, autonomous demand for goods and services; and, assume that a decrease in EQ serves to exacerbate income inequality but, conceivably, to augment autonomous demand. Overall, the identity for aggregate demand then could be written as:

$$DG = \overline{DG} + dEQ + iI + bY, \qquad (4)$$

where, once more, Y is national income (output) and I is the level of indebtedness. The substantive interpretation of equation (4) is that $\overline{\text{DG}}$ is some positive, fixed demand for goods and services embodying autonomous consumer, investor and government spending; $i \geq 0$: indebtedness possibly stimulates the demand for domestically produced goods and services at rate i, $\frac{\partial \text{DG}}{\partial I} = i \geq 0$; b is the spending propensity relative to current national income, Y, $\frac{\partial \text{DG}}{\partial Y} = b$ where $0 < b < 1$; and $d \leq 0$: to the extent that wealth is more equitably distributed and EQ is of large magnitude, the effect of autonomous demand, $\overline{\text{DG}}$, is diminished by an amount dEQ so that $\frac{\partial \text{DG}}{\partial \text{EQ}} = d \leq 0$. Thus, in this formulation, if there is no income transfer, EQ = 0, the spending propensity associated with national income level Y would give rise to an aggregate demand of $(\overline{\text{DG}} + \text{bY})$ which exceeds demand under a nonzero income transfer, EQ > 0, (DG + bY − |d|EQ). For example, suppose two countries are identical in all respects except that $EQ_1 > EQ_2$. Then, clearly, $(\overline{\text{DG}} + \text{bY} − |d|EQ_2) > (\overline{\text{DG}} + \text{bY} − |d|EQ_1)$, and we know that the income transfers of the second results in greater aggregate demand. Hirschman describes the "conventional wisdom" regarding the sign of d in the following way:

> Since only the better-off people are in a position to acquire the automobiles, houses, or apartments, and many of the consumer durables, the increase in income that comes with economic expansion must be channelled to them. The poorer sections are at a hopeless distance from being customers of the expanding industries and would merely "waste" any increased earnings on rice and beans; their income must therefore be kept from increasing, and more so as the latter items are in inelastic supply. But in order to achieve that sort of consumption profile (also designated as "excluding and concentrating development" — *desarrollo excluyente y concentrador)*, political repression and authoritarianism are required (Hirschman, 1979:81).

[The above formula is admittedly unsatisfactory. It may be better to assume that the effect of income transfers is to diminish the aggregate spending propensity out of national income (EQ.bY where $0 < \text{EQ} < 1$) rather than to posit the effect of income transfers entirely on (total) autonomous demand (cf. Feder's (1982) assumption that government sets parameters affecting import-substitution and other variables; cf. also Taylor's model (1979: ch. 3) for studying the effects of Egyptian food subsidies in which government sets investment and income distribution parameters). Also, it should be noted that, in this monograph, it is assumed that the level of government spending is essentially fixed and that fiscal policy is one of the tools regimes use to accomplish the larger objective of encouraging an uneven expansion of consumption. However, it is important that eventually deficit spending and related practices be taken into account inasmuch as such policies also have important political-economic impacts that affect patterns of indebted economic growth. See, for instance, Geithman (1974) and Ames (1979). See chapter 5 for alternative approaches to modeling the effects of income (re)maldistribution.]

Consider the situation in which authorities decide to fix income transfers at some EQ'. What are the ramifications of such a policy for indebtedness and output? If the goods market is in equilibrium under the policy, EQ', national output, Y, exactly matches aggregate demands, DG. Equation (4) then can be rewritten:

$$\begin{aligned}
Y = DG = & \quad \overline{DG} + dEQ + iI + bY \\
(1 - b)Y = & \quad \overline{DG} + dEQ + iI \\
Y = & \quad \tfrac{1}{1-b}\,[\overline{DG} + dEQ + iI].
\end{aligned} \tag{5}$$

Equation (5) indicates that with income transfers fixed at EQ' the goods market "clears" under a variety of indebtedness and output combinations. More specifically, setting transfers equal to EQ' allows for all the equilibrium combinations, (I, Y), along the *state reform line, SR line,* in figure 5. For instance, the goods market is in equilibrium under policy EQ' at ξ_1 since with indebtedness at I_1 and income at Y_1, aggregate demand, DG_1, is exactly equal to the output (supply) of goods and services, Y_1. Higher levels of indebtedness augment demand for domestically produced goods and services. Hence, under the same policy, EQ', such levels of indebtedness as I_2 are associated with the comparatively higher output, Y_2; the demand for and supply of goods and services are in equilibrium at ξ_2.

The 45° line in the upper graphs of the figures represents the condition of national output (supply) matching aggregate demand. For example, at ξ_2 we have

$$DG_2 = \overline{DG} + iI_2 + bY_2 + dEQ',$$

which exactly matches the output, Y_2, by virtue of the intersection of the 45° line and the aggregate demand line for DG_2. Thus, at this equilibrium we have

$$Y_2 = (\tfrac{1}{1-b})(iI_2 + \overline{DG} + dEQ).$$

Connecting all these equilibrium pairs of indebtedness and output

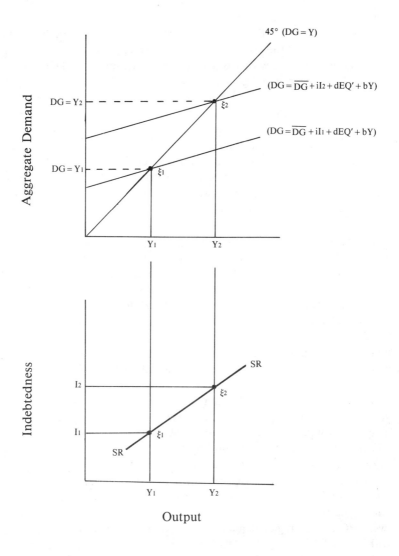

Figure 5. The SR Line Under the Policy of Fixing Income Transfers at EQ′

Note. The 45° line in the top diagram represents the goods market equilibrium where the supply of goods and services equals aggregate demand; DG = Y.

generates the state reform line for income transfer policy EQ′. [To review, along the state reform line are those combinations of indebtedness and output which clear the goods market under the policy of fixing income transfers at EQ′ (and with fixed autonomous demands of $\overline{DG}$). Along the SR line the supply of goods and services exactly matches aggregate demand. The positive slope of the SR line derives from the fact that higher indebtedness may stimulate demand for domestic goods. Hence a higher I is associated with a higher output. Lower indebtedness may create comparatively less demand for domestically produced goods and services and therefore the equilibrium output level is lower.]

Observe from equation (5) that for this second kind of state intermediation, the equilibrium relation between indebtedness and output depends on the quotient, $\frac{i}{1-b}$. When the stimulative effects of indebtedness and the propensity to spend current income are both relatively great, a slightly larger I is associated with a much larger output since significantly more goods and services are needed to satisfy the ensuing (externally financed) augmentation of aggregate demand and the increased spending which results from higher income. *Put another way, if i is much larger than (1 – b), the state reform line will be relatively flat.* On the other hand, *if* indebtedness has very little effect on domestic spending and the propensity to spend current income is relatively low *[(1-b) > >i]*, increased indebtedness is not associated with a significantly higher output. Rather, a higher level of indebtedness is associated with only a slightly larger level of output and *the state reform line is quite steep.*

If there is some truth to the claim that income transfers diminish total autonomous demand, i.e., $d \neq 0$, the effect of attempts to redress social inequality will alter the combinations of indebtedness and ouput under which the goods market is in equilibrium. Hence the position of the state reform line will change. In particular, *a change in income transfers from EQ′ to some fixed EQ″ > EQ′ shifts the SR line to the northwest* while *a reduction in income transfer to some fixed EQ‴ < EQ′ shifts the SR line to the southeast.* Since there presumably is an inverse relation between EQ and aggregate demand, the decision to redress social inequality with EQ″ > EQ′ means that DG is reduced by $|dEQ''| > |dEQ'|$. Accordingly, under the more reform-oriented policy, EQ″, the equilibrium level of output corresponding to any given level of indebtedness is lower than that which obtains when the policy is EQ′; and the state reform line shifts to the northwest (figure 6). On the basis of the same kind of reasoning, it follows that reduction in income transfers to some EQ‴ < EQ′ moves the state reform line to the southeast where higher levels of output are associated with each level of indebtedness by virtue of the less severe

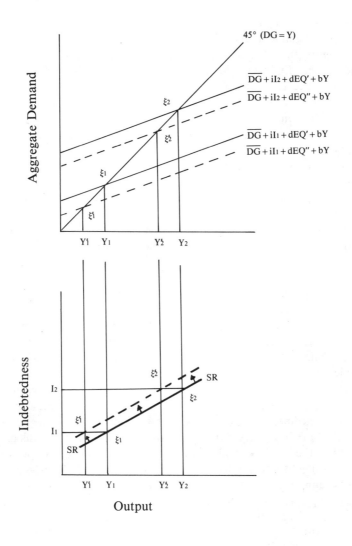

Figure 6. Effects of a Shift in Reform Policy — Increasing Income
Transfers to Some Fixed Level EQ″ > EQ′

45

retardation of aggregate demand under EQ'''.

Regarding indebtedness and output combinations off the state reform line (figure 7), note that at E_1 we have an indebtedness level of I_2 which under policy EQ' would be in equilibrium if output were Y_2. But at E_1, the output level is only Y_1, hence we know that the stimulative effects of I_2 are not being matched by an adequate supply of goods and services. In general, then, *there is an excess of demand for goods and services when indebtedness and output are above the state reform line.* The opposite applies — *there is an excess supply of goods and services* — *when (I, Y) is below the state reform line.* At E_2, we have a relatively low level of indebtedness which corresponds to a smaller, external stimulus for domestic purchases. With indebtedness at I_1, the market would be in equilibrium if output were Y_1. However, at E_2, output is $Y_2 > Y_1$, hence the production of goods and services exceeds total aggregate demand.

In the present formulation, government's posture toward the reform function is embodied in policies designed to transfer income from upper to lower income groups. These transfers affect the conditions under which the goods market clears. The indebtedness-output equilibria corresponding to this situation (in which the demand for and supply of goods and services are equal) are represented by the positively sloped state reform or SR line. The steepness of that line depends on the relative impact that indebtedness has on the demands for domestically produced goods and services, and also on the relative propensity to spend out of current national income, Y; if $d \neq 0$, the policy of fixing income transfers at higher levels, EQ'' > EQ', shifts the state reform line to the northwest while reductions in income transfers shift the state reform line to the southeast; and, for a policy of fixed income transfers, EQ', combinations of I and Y above the SR line imply an excess demand for goods and services whereas indebtedness-output combinations below the SR line connote an excess supply (output) of goods and services.

This completes the analysis of how each policy, in isolation, affects (is related to) levels of indebtedness and output.

JOINT POLICY EQUILIBRIA: INDEBTED ECONOMIC GROWTH EXPLAINED

Just as the interplay between the entrepreneurial and reform functions of economic development explains the recent change in the character of foreign investment, the *joint* formulation of entrepreneurship and income transfer policies accounts for current patterns of indebted economic growth. Decisions regarding income transfers, EQ, affect aggregate

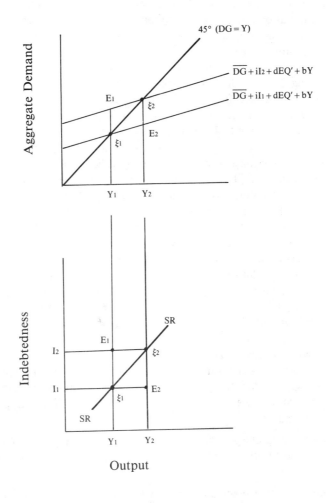

Figure 7. Combinations of Indebtedness and Output
Which Lie off the SR Line

demand, equation (4), and in that way alter the nature of goods market equilibria. The goods market, in turn, determines national output. Hence, the fortunes of native firms may be directly affected by income transfers. But demands of entrepreneurial support and substitution depend, in part, on the fortunes of national enterprise. So indirectly, through the nY term in equation (1), income transfers have an impact on government's relations with national enterprise; specifically, on the effectiveness of prevailing policies of state entrepreneurship. Similarly, by providing assistance to native firms, authorities encourage greater indebtedness, which, through the iI term in equation (4), conceivably alters the level of aggregate demand. Accordingly, even under a fixed income transfer policy, entrepreneurial support and substitution can promote economic growth through the externally financed (publicly guaranteed) augmentation of demand. [To the extent that entrepreneurial assistance and substitution promote growth which, by its very nature, reinforces income inequality (Frank and Webb, 1977; Sheahan, 1980), state entrepreneurship may offset the effects of income redistribution policy.] Thus, patterns of indebted economic growth are a consequence of the interactive effects both of governmental intervention in the goods market *and* governmental relations with native entrepreneurs. Or, in terms of the diagrammatic representation, the key to understanding how mixes of state entrepreneurship and income transfers shape histories of indebted economic growth lies in the interrelationship of those equilibrium conditions that define the SE and SR lines.

In order to demonstrate how such an explanation can be constructed, I make two stylized assumptions about how levels of indebtedness and output adjust when the goods market is out of equilibrium and/or the demands of native enterprise are not in balance with the entrepreneurial support and substitution the state is providing:

Assumption A. Output expands when there is an excess demand for goods and services; output contracts when there is an excess supply of goods and services.

Assumption B. Indebtedness falls when there is an excess demand for state entrepreneurship; indebtedness increases when there is an excess of entrepreneurial support and substitution being offered by the state.

Assumption (A), which departs from structuralist formulations that see Southern output purely as a function of supply and that posit Southern growth rates to be determined by Northern growth rates (Taylor, 1981), appears reasonable for the market-oriented countries we are studying. Also, recall that the model applies to the current stage of economic

48

development in indebted countries; it is plausible to assume that as inventories become depleted, some local firms will be capable of increasing output. [Implicit here is the presumption of fixed prices.] The presumption underlying assumption (B) is that, in the aggregate, the availability of foreign capital varies on the basis of the state's response to the demands for entrepreneurial support and substitution from local enterprise. When the state is unwilling to provide all the assistance that native firms demand (DE > SE'), lending is curtailed in response to the lack of public guarantees for new loans and/or the fact that the excess demands for state entrepreneurship are a consequence of a decline in national output. (Note that, conceivably, the condition DE > SE' captures the effects of government's attempts to ameliorate social inequality. Policies that increase income transfers may also reduce aggregate demand if d < 0. This, in turn, could lead to more requests for entrepreneurial support and substitution and thus cause an excess of demands, DE > SE'.) Conversely, an excess of state entrepreneurship is being offered, SE' > DE, public guarantees for foreign borrowing are available and/or the credit-worthiness of national enterprise may be enhanced by an increase in output and concomitant decline in the needs of native entrepreneurs. Hence international lenders offer capital on easier terms and I increase. [I assume that governments are authoritarian in the way they manage the reform function and that the (credit) supply conditions of the 1970s apply. The availability of foreign capital then can be taken as a given as in assumption (B). Also, it is important to stress that assumption (B) applies to the aggregate level of indebtedness. To be sure, international lenders still exercise circumspection in deciding which firms will obtain easier terms and exactly what those terms will be.]

Since the slope of both equilibrium relations (lines) corresponding to the two kinds of state intermediation are non-negative, four possible cases must be considered; [1] the slope of the state reform (SR) line exceeds that of the state entrepreneurship (SE) line; [2] the slope of the SE line exceeds that of the SR line; [3] the slopes of the two lines are identical but their indebtedness (I) intercepts are different — SR and SE do not intersect (there are no mutual equilibrium combinations of indebtedness and output); and [4] the slopes and the I-intercepts are identical — SE and SR are the same lines.

Case (1) would appear to represent the most substantively meaningful account of indebted economic growth.

Appendix A shows that case (1) is equivalent to the condition $[(1 - b)k > i|n|]$. Since we know that increased indebtedness usually breeds more demand for state entrepreneurship and that growth normally does not have any *major* impact on the demand for entrepreneurial support and substitution, it would seem reasonable to assume that in most countries k is larger than $|n|$. More important, there is much evidence to suggest that I has little impact on the demand for domestically produced goods and services. In fact, often indebtedness is incurred in the form of supplier credits and/or with obligations to purchase foreign-made goods and technologies (Perez, 1980:149; Gillis, 1980:278; Choksi, 1979:46-47). Hence the coefficient i is likely to be quite small and the slope of SR will exceed that of SE.

This situation is depicted in figure 8, where ξ^*:(I^*,Y^*) is the equilibrium combination of indebtedness and output which obtains under the policy of (jointly) fixing income transfers at EQ' and state entrepreneurship at SE'. At ξ^*, the goods market clears (DG = Y) and, simultaneously, the demands for entrepreneurial support and substitution are satisfied (DE = SE'). In addition, it can be shown that given any initial breakdown of indebtedness and output which is not identical to (I^*,Y^*), under policy (EQ',SE'), the economy will adjust to ξ^*. For example, consider the combination, E_0:(I_0,Y_0), in figure 8. E_0 is above the state reform line and below the state entrepreneurship line. From what we learned above, this means that at E_0 there is an excess demand for goods and services (DG > Y) and, at the same time, the state is willing to provide more entrepreneurial assistance than national enterprise demands (SE' > DE). Under the adjustment assumptions, then, local firms increase output and international lenders make available more resources for borrowing by national enterprise; those funds, in turn, further stimulate aggregate demand (albeit, to only a limited degree, given the relatively small magnitude of i in this case). The growth in output has some beneficial impact on native enterprise so the demand for state entrepreneurship subsequently declines somewhat. However, since k undoubtedly is larger then $|n|$ (see above), the greater indebtedness is associated with a net increase in the demands national enterprise places on the state by virtue of its even greater financial obligations. What the diagram tells us is that, eventually, these countervailing forces exactly balance one another at (I^*,Y^*). Hence, at ξ^*, no further alterations in the levels of indebtedness and output are forthcoming. Finally, this equilibrium mix of indebtedness and output depends both on the prevailing income transfer policy, EQ', and government's willingness to offer entrepreneurial support and substitute for native enterprise, or SE'. This also is clear from the expression for ξ^*, which contains both policies (see Appendix A):

$$I^* = [\frac{(1-b)}{k(1-b)-i|n|}][SE' - \overline{DE} + \frac{|n|}{(1-b)}(\overline{DG} + dEQ')]$$

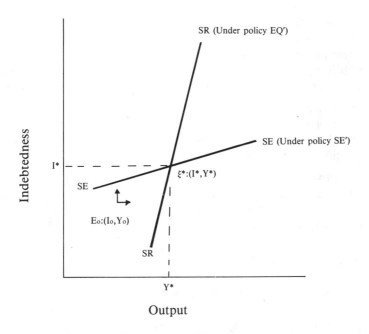

Figure 8. Indebtedness-Output Equilibrium Under Entrepreneurial Assistance-Income Transfer Policy Mix, (SE′,EQ′), With Illustrative Adjustment From Initial Indebtedness-Output Combination at E_0.

$$Y^* = [\tfrac{k}{k(1-b)-b|n|}][\overline{DG} + \tfrac{i}{k}(SE' - \overline{DE}) + dEQ'].$$

Having seen how indebtedness and output depend on a fixed mix of governmental policies, the next question which must be addressed is: of what consequence are decisions to *alter* policies of state entrepreneurship and/or income transfers? The implications of the diagrammatic analysis are as follows — recall that our discussion applies to the type of political economies where $[(1-b)k > i|n|]$:

Consequence 1

When state entrepreneurship is unchanged at some (fixed) SE′, and attempts to ameliorate social inequality affect aggregate demand (d < 0), a shift in income transfers from EQ′ to some fixed EQ″ > EQ′ results in comparatively lower indebtedness and lower output.

51

Consequence 2
When state entrepreneurship is unchanged at some (fixed) SE', and attempts to ameliorate social inequality affect aggregate demand (d < 0), a shift in income transfers from EQ' to some fixed EQ" < EQ' results in a comparatively greater level of indebtedness and higher output.

Consequence 3
When income transfers are unchanged at some (fixed) EQ' (or d = 0), an increased commitment to state entrepreneurship (a shift to some SE" > SE') results in comparatively greater indebtedness and higher output.

Consequence 4
When income transfers are unchanged at some (fixed) EQ' (or d = 0), a reduction in state entrepreneurship (a shift to some SE''' < SE') results in comparatively lower indebtedness and lower output.

Consider, for example, consequence (3) (figure 9). By assumption (B) the offer of increased entrepreneurial support and substitution results in more borrowing by native firms and hence in an augmentation of indebtedness. In addition, the shift to SE" > SE' means that the demands of native firms are not satisfied; and, there is a new SE line which lies to the northwest of the original state entrepreneurship line (figure 3). So, if output were to remain fixed at some Y*, the government's new-found readiness to assist national enterprise would eventually lead to greater indebtedness at some Ī, where authorities would be meeting the demands for entrepreneurial support and substitution. (This hypothetical case of a fixed Y* is used for purposes of illustration. In reality, the shift to SE" would lead to changes both in I and in Y, for the reasons given in the discussion that follows.) But, with income transfers unchanged at EQ', the pair (Ī,Y*) lies above the state reform line so the goods market would not be in equilibrium: there would be an insufficient supply of goods and services by virtue of the increases in indebtedness having (marginally) stimulated aggregate demand. So, under assumption (A), output would increase, thereby benefiting native firms and making possible even greater increases in indebtedness, until finally, a new equilibrium obtains at ξ**. Thus, the government's new-found commitment to entrepreneurial support and substitution (alone) results in some (I**,Y**), which implies both greater indebtedness and economic growth. This is consequence (3).

These results provide the basis for understanding how current patterns of indebted economic growth depend on *sequences of policies* adopted by entreprenerial-authoritarian governments. Each shift in policy — each change in the mix of state entrepreneurship and income transfer — results in different indebtedness/output equilibria, according to the magnitude

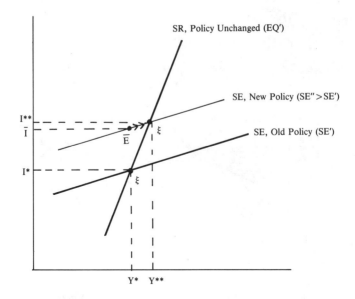

Figure 9. Diagrammatic Derivation of Consequence (3): The Impact of Increased State Entrepreneurial Assistance When Income Transfers Are Unchanged

and direction of governmental intermediation and the prevailing political-economic conditions; that is, the values of b,d,i,n,$\overline{DG}$, and $\overline{DE}$ in each country. Observed records of indebted economic growth are the outcomes of this "unfolding" of entrepreneurial-authoritarian intermediation. Where the policy sequence entails steady increases in entrepreneurial support and substitution coupled with a reduction in income transfers, the state reform line gradually moves to the southeast, the state entrepreneurship line shifts to the northwest, and the pattern of indebted economic growth resembles that in figure 10. In contrast, if authorities reverse their policies, ameliorating some social inequities for a brief period and/or momentarily refusing to assist the entrepreneurial function, the SR and SE lines, at times, will shift in both directions and the pattern will resemble that in figures 11 or 12. In this way, then, that government's involvement in the two functions of economic growth accounts for the trends in indebtedness and output.

Returning to the questions posed earlier with respect to the Latin

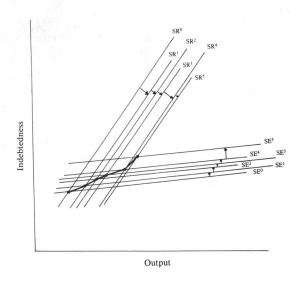

Figure 10. Outcome of Illustrative Policy Sequence Where Entrepreneurial Assistance Constantly Increases and Income Transfers Steadily Are Reduced

Note: Formally, SR^t corresponds to the SR line when income transfers vary from $EQ^0 > \ldots > EQ^5$ and SE^t corresponds to the SE line when assistance is adjusted as follows: $SE^0 < \ldots < SE^5$, $t = 0, \ldots, 5$.

American experience, on the basis of the diagrammatic argument, one would *hypothesize* that the regimes in Brazil, Peru and Colombia effectively did pursue an equivalent sequence of entrepreneurial-(re)distributive intermediation. We would expect that for all three countries, entrepreneurial support and substitution has gradually increased while, at the same time, relatively little has been done to ameliorate social inequality. Since the political-economic conditions are not identical in these cases, we would not expect the rate of indebted growth to be the same. For instance, it is likely that the impact of indebtedness on aggregate demand (the i coefficient) is of different magnitude in the three countries; one would conjecture that the Brazilian state reform line is the flattest of the three, for example. But, in general, the policies pursued

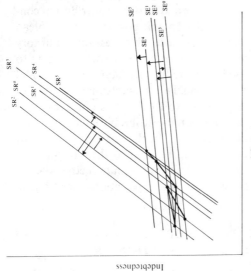

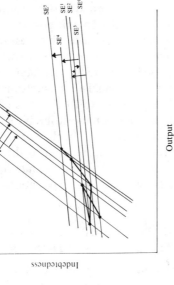

Output

Figure 11. Outcome of Illustrative Policy Sequence Where Entrepreneurial Assistance Is Both Increased and Decreased (State Entrepreneurship Policy Reversal) While Income Transfers Are Progressively Reduced (Policy of Promoting Social Inequality; $d \neq 0$)

Output

Figure 12. Outcome of Illustrative Policy Sequence In Which Entrepreneurial Assistance is Both Increased and Decreased While Income Transfers Are Both Increased and Decreased (Policy Reversals In Both Types of State Intermediation)

Note. The reversal in entrepreneurial assistance occurs between t2 and t3 so that $SE^0 < SE^3 = SE^1 = SE^3 = SE^1$ so that $SE^4 < SE^2$.

55

by the three governments might have been roughly equivalent in that the mixes of state entrepreneurship assistance and income redistribution contributed to similar patterns of indebted economic growth. In the Chilean case, the *hypothesis* would be that the chaotic indebtedness-output history is due to reversals in state entrepreneurship coupled with attempts to redress and then to exacerbate social inequality [cf. figures 1 (Chile) and 12]. In other words, the diagrammatic analysis suggests that the Chilean experience — at least in the period prior to 1973 — is an outgrowth of a rather peculiar sequence of entrepreneurial-distributive intermediation, a portion of which entailed policy reversals. In chapter 4 the validity of some of these hypotheses are assessed in relation to the Brazilian experience. Chapter 5 contains some observations about whether the experiences of the other countries conform to the expectations derived here.

FURTHER IMPLICATIONS: POLICY OPTIONS AND THE LIMITS OF STATE INTERMEDIATION

Many Third World governments have been or are actively engaged in some form of planning (ECLA, 1964; Fitzgerald, 1976). And, public authorities almost always have economic goals, especially with respect to economic growth. What does the diagrammatic representation tell us about government's abilities to achieve desired levels of output?

Suppose that a government's desired output is Y_{target} and the prevailing output level is some Y_o corresponding to the policy mix which yields the lines SR^o and SE^o in figure 13. Then, the model indicates that there are numerous, equally effective policies, all of which produce the desired level of output, Y_{target}. To be specific, a government's options vary from drastically reducing income transfers — shifting *only* the state reform from SR^o to SR^f — to offering substantially more entrepreneurial assistance to native enterprise, shifting *only* the state entrepreneurship line from SE^o to SE^d. In between, so to speak, are a variety of equally effective policies such as shifts to (SR^a, SE^a), (SR^b, SE^b) and (SE^c, SR^c). [Still other options are (1) shifting SE^o to the southeast (decreasing entrepreneurial assistance) and moving SR^o beyond SR^f (promoting severe income concentration), and (2) adopting a series of shifts leading up to one of those depicted in figure 13. Feder (1982) carries out his analysis for a moving GDP target; obviously, this analysis could be extended to allow for such a possibility with the same basic result.]

Under all of these policy combinations the output target is achieved. Thus, at least in terms of growth, various policy mixes are interchangeable; they all serve the government's growth objectives equally well.

56

The policies differ, of course, in their effect on indebtedness. Associated with each option — each possible shift in the state entrepreneurship and/or state reform lines — is a different indebtedness outcome. If we posit a target level of indebtedness as well, the number of alternatives is drastically reduced. In fact, when authorities seek to achieve multiple objectives (I_{target}, Y_{target}), they have only one option, namely, to adopt that (single) mix of entrepreneurial assistance and income redistribution which simultaneously shifts the SE^o line to some $\overline{SE}$ and the SR^o line to some $\overline{SR}$ (figure 14). Any other policy does not accomplish such shifts in SE and SR and will fail to achieve the target levels of indebtedness and output.

These results suggest, first, that two governments may be attempting to accomplish the same goal with respect to economic growth, even though they enact quite different kinds of policies. Put another way, the fact that two growth-oriented governments employ different mixes of state entrepreneurship and income redistribution does not necessarily mean their policies aren't motivated by the same output objective. Second, the diagrammatic analysis underscores the importance of ideology and other contextual factors of Third World political economies. For it is clear that such factors have much to do with the choice of one possibly equally effective mix of state entrepreneurship and income redistribution over another. For example, it appears that, *ceteris paribus*, Chilean decision makers might pursue policy options that entailed less entrepreneurial assistance because of their commitment to a free market ideology (cf. Cardoso, 1979:52-53).

For regimes that pursue multiple objectives, there is no set of equally effective policy options. Rather, if both the indebtedness and output targets are to be achieved, government has only one choice. The task becomes that of ascertaining or "learning to identify" this best mix of state entrepreneurship and income redistribution. The learning capability of Third World governments therefore should be an important source of variation in states' policies (ECLA, 1964:181; Evans, 1979:45; Aronson, 1977). In fact, to the extent that the sanctioning of social inequality is a necessary, complementary form of intermediation ($d <$ 0), differences in learning capability could account for the contradictory findings regarding the impact of entrepreneurial substitution (Tyler, 1974; Churchill, 1974). That is, the success of the state's commercial ventures could depend on governments recognizing the need to complement entrepreneurial substitution with various degrees of income redistribution (if entrepreneurial assistance alone would not achieve growth targets).

Externally imposed constraints on borrowing may also reduce the number of options available to Third World governments. Few, if any,

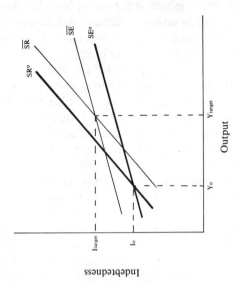

Figure 14. The Single Policy Which Achieves Indebted Economic Growth Target (I_{target}, Y_{target})

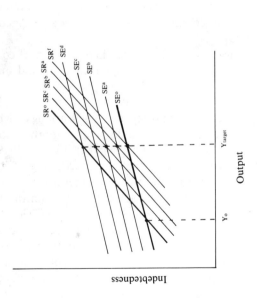

Figure 13. Policy Options When A Regime Is Interested *Only* In Increasing Output From Y_o to Y_{target}

58

past attempts at modeling indebted economic growth address the possibility of externally imposed constraints. For instance, Feder (1982) assumes an essentially unlimited supply of foreign funds (and boom growth in exports). Nor do Morley and Smith (1973) allow for external constraints on the growth rate of investment. As we will see, there are important substantive reasons to include this eventuality in any analysis of indebted economic growth.

If countries are constrianed in the level of indebtedness they can incur, governments may have only one choice in terms of how much entrepreneurial assistance they need to offer to achieve Y_{target}. For instance, suppose that the I_{target} in figure 14 had been set by some external authority. Then, if the government's output objective were Y_{target}, the shift to $\overline{SE}$ and $\overline{SR}$ would have been, in part, the outcome of the external imposition of the constraint on indebtedness. But, what if the same external authority dictates further constraints, on the policy options themselves? If, for example, the maximum level of indebtedness is externally dictated and government is forced to reduce entrepreneurial support and substitution so that the SE line moves to the southeast (figure 15), the achievement of the output objective will require a comparatively greater shift in the state reform line, far to the southeast. Hence external constraints on I and on the policy options themselves may translate into quite severe tradeoffs between social inequality and growth.

It has, so far, been presumed that authorities comprehend the workings of the political economy, and that the problem of achieving indebted economic growth essentially is one of ascertaining the appropriate mix of state entrepreneurship and income redistribution. But suppose that political-economic relationships are misunderstood. For instance, of what consequence is the possibility that the effects of income redistribution on aggregate demand is nil?

Of particular interest is Serra's (1979) evaluation of the inevitability of superexploitation thesis — the idea that "authoritarianism is an essential instrument for guaranteeing capitalist accumulation, i.e., a means of preventing the working class from jeopardizing or frustrating the realization of superexploitation through its organizations and its protests." He agrees that restrictions on political freedom contribute to the concentration of income among certain groups. And he admits that inequitable forms of income redistribution indeed may contribute to the rapid growth of certain sectors of developing economies. But Serra takes issue with the claim that the expansion of these same sectors is required for the development of the economy as a whole and therefore that restrictions on political rights and sanctions on social equality are necessary evils of

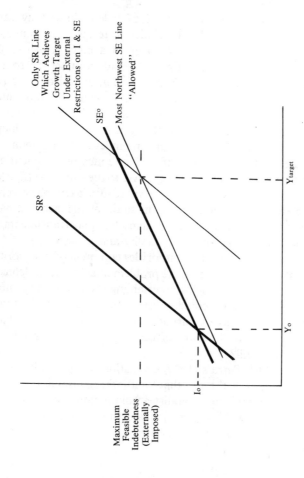

Figure 15. The Policy Option When There Are External Constraints On The Maximum Indebtedness Which May Be Incurred and On the Maximum Entrepreneurial Assistance Which Can Be Offered To Native Enterprise

delayed industrialization:

> I do not deny that in an underdeveloped economy a pattern of growth
> that emphasizes consumer durables will tend to restrict the possibilities
> for direct or indirect income redistribution (in this case through the
> "social expenditures" of the state), or that it will contribute to a
> greater concentration of income. Yet considering the case of Brazil,
> there is no reason to suppose that, simply because of its capacity to
> change demand curves and to create new financing for consumption,
> the consumer goods sector *had* to grow at an annual rate of 20
> percent. It seems to me that, in large part, the growth of this sector
> also responded to the concentration of income that derived from "ex-
> ogenous" factors, such as the repression of unions and the political
> weakness of the popular sector... And there was no reason to sup-
> pose that the survival or restoration of political freedoms, including
> those relating to the contractural power of the unions, is *necessarily*
> an impediment to the survival of the system because of the implacable
> logic of certain "laws" that govern "dependent capitalism" — laws
> which, as long as this system endures, would leave us no option other
> than living under a bureaucratic-authoritarian regime (Serra,
> 1979:110-11).

Serra's analysis and that of others (Morley and Smith, 1973; Frank
and Webb, 1977: chp. 2, n. 7) suggest that even at lower to moderate
levels of economic development, social inequality may not necessarily
contribute to economic growth or, formally, that the value of the d
coefficient in equation (4) may be zero. The diagrammatic representation gives us some indication of what such an eventuality would mean
for the effectiveness of government's (entrepreneurial-distributive)
policies. Recall that reductions in income transfers are believed to shift
the state reform line to the southeast. If d is effectively zero, income
redistribution — a change in EQ — has no effect on the position of the
SR line; the equilibrium relation for the goods market is fixed, regardless
of income transfers. It follows that attempts to achieved indebtedness-
output targets like those in figure 14 will invariably fail by virtue of there
being an (inappropriate) insufficient level of entrepreneurial assistance
offered by the government. Or, more fundamentally, it will be impossible to accomplish (I_{target}, Y_{target}) when the position of the state reform
line is fixed. Thus, in figure 16, the shift in the state entrepreneurship
line to SE is intended to achieve indebted economic growth corresponding to (I_{target}, Y_{target}). But, in reality, the change in income transfers has
no effect on the position of the state reform line and the outcome is ($\overline{I}, \overline{Y}$).
Moreover, even if authorities realize that the position of the state reform
line is unaffected by its policy choice (EQ), they still cannot achieve their
goal (I_{target}, Y_{target}) because shifts in the state entrepreneurship line alone

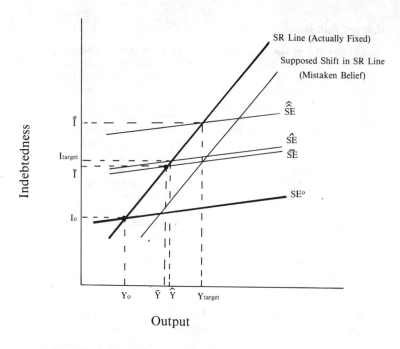

Figure 16. The Consequence of a Mistaken Belief In the Effects of Income Transfer $(d \approx 0)$

are inadequate for this purpose. A change to $\hat{SE}$ will yield I_{target} but not Y_{target}; a move to $\hat{\hat{SE}}$ will yield Y_{target} but not I_{target}. In sum, the consequences of a mistaken belief about the necessity for social inequality can lead to poor performance with respect to the achievement of indebted economic growth objectives and also, perhaps, to an even more inequitable distribution of wealth, denying some citizens their basic economic needs.

4

BRAZIL: A CASE STUDY

According to the diagrammatic analysis, the history of indebtedness and output in Brazil is an outgrowth of the state reform line having shifted to the southeast, while the state entrepreneurship line simultaneously shifted to the northwest. Brazilian governments apparently adopted a sequence of policy mixes designed to exacerbate income inequality and to increase entrepreneurial assistance and substitution. This hypothesis implies that a policy of wage controls and reduced social services augmented aggregate demand and enhanced Brazil's credit-worthiness to international lenders; at the same time, state entrepreneurship not only placated nationalist elements of the military, bureaucracy and local business community, but also, in the context of a "closed" political system, actually stimulated domestic capital accumulation.

There is little doubt that the government systematically suppressed unions. Even the World Bank study (Pfefferman and Webb, 1979:64-65) acknowledges the effect of minimum wage legislation on workers in the unionized firms included in the DIESSE surveys. (See Alves, 1982b for an extended discussion of governmental control over unions and wages.) Pfefferman and Webb also maintain that, in comparison to 1960, fewer Brazilians are below the poverty line, and that life expectancy has become more equitable. However, data collected by Alves (1982a,b) suggest that social inequality has become increasingly more pronounced and that this is partly attributable to a *decline* in the share of governmental spending on basic social services (table 1).

Indeed, Pfefferman and Webb (1979:103) acknowledge the "lag in public services" and also the high levels of malnutrition and infant mortality (see also Bacha and Taylor, 1980). In this context, it should also be pointed out that Alves's (1982a:21) evidence for the prevalence of child labor suggests a reason why Pfefferman and Webb (1979:8) reached different conclusions about trends in inequality when they

Table 1

Total Percentage of National Budget Allotted to Ministries of Health and Education for Years 1965-1974

HEALTH		EDUCATION	
Year	Percentage	Year	Percentage
1965	---	1965	11.07
1966	4.29	1966	9.70
1967	3.45	1967	8.71
1968	2.71	1968	7.74
1969	2.59	1969	8.69
1970	1.79	1970	7.33
1971	1.53	1971	6.78
1972	1.24	1972	5.62
1973	1.09	1973	5.21
1974	0.99	1974	4.95

Source: Senator Franco Montoro, *DA "Democracia" que Temos Para a Democracia que Queremos* (Rio de Janeiro: Editora Paz e Terra, 1974:6,7). Printed by permission.

looked at *household income*. [Two caveats are in order here. First, there is some evidence of minor reversals in the Brazilian government's redistributive polices and, of course, also of changes in the nature of interest group intermediation (Alves, 1982a:833, chart 11.1). Second, as noted above, there is much evidence that the corporate decisions of Brazilian state enterprises served to exacerbate income inequality as well as to make reprivatization — policy reversals in state entrepreneurship — more difficult to accomplish over time (Baer and Figueroa, 1981; Mendonca de Barros and Graham, 1978; Bacha, 1976).]

This account of the Brazilian government's policies is consistent with arguments of both its detractors and defenders. Critics point to the political restrictions imposed by government decrees of the 1960s and also to trends in social inequality to indicate that indebted economic growth has been promoted by a "state which specifically places national security above the individual rights and security of its citizens, and, further, that "The anatomy of (Brazil's) National Security State is thus a coordinated program to limit the rights of all citizens" (Alves, 1982a:5). These detractors usually do not question the motivation for state entrepreneurship, or doubt the effects of income inequality on aggregate demand. Rather, they deplore the consequences of entrepreneurial-redistributive intermediation; the continued (indirect) reliance on foreign capital and technology by native firms (state companies account for 70% of Brazil's foreign debt) and the inequities that lower socioeconomic groups in Brazilian society must bear for the sake of economic growth (*Latin American Regional Reports* RB-82-08, 17 September 1982).

As pointed out in chapter 2, Brazilian policy makers and international financial community members usually see these policies and their outcomes as necessary, short-term evils, and that, given the lateness of Brazil's economic development, restrictions on political rights and promotion of social inequality are the only means by which growth can be achieved. External sources of capital can (should) be secured only if lenders believe government can withstand social and economic pressures for the kind of income redistribution which would supposedly reduce aggregate demand and hence retard economic development. Similarly, planners and state managers believe they must be insulated from partisan demands if the economy is to be managed (operated) in a manner that promotes growth and makes debt servicing possible. As a manager of a government firm told McDonough (1980) some years ago:

> In an underdeveloped country, the population is solely concerned with its own survival. It does not have the objective or subjective conditions to be worried about other things and to engage consciously in politics. Therefore, social and political development of the sophisticated kind, what you might call "political liberty" for the privileged classes, ought to be sacrificed temporarily so that with economic development we can generate wealth and overcome this phase (McDonough, 1980:548; see also Alberts and Brundeis, 1978).

Proponents of the Brazilian experience insist that the hypothesized shifts in state reform and state entrepreneurship lines represent the successful implementation of the only feasible strategy Brazil had in the 1960s and 1970s.

Since this account of Brazil's indebted economic growth is so widely accepted, it would be easy to conclude that underlying the corresponding pattern in figure 1 (Brazil) is a sequence of entrepreneurial-redistributive intermediation, seen in figure 10. However, there is another explanation for the gradual increase in indebtedness and output that Brazil (and other countries) have experienced. Recall that one implication of the diagrammatic analysis is that a growth target, Y_{target}, could be achieved solely by shifting the state entrepreneurship line to the northwest (figure 13). Also, notice in figure 16 that if income inequality has essentially no impact on aggregate demand (d is effectively zero, so the state reform line is essentially fixed) and government can ignore the indebtedness target, I$_{target}$, Y$_{target}$ can be achieved by shifting SE^{o} to SE. This suggests that, contrary to both detractors' and defenders' suppositions, indebted economic growth has been more an outgrowth of externally financed state entrepreneurship than a result of the state's willingness and ability to serve as entrepreneur *and* simultaneously tolerate (promote) income inequality. Authoritarian politics may well have enhanced the profitability of native enterprise. For example, in contrast to the situation prior to the 1964 coup, Brazilian state firms have been able to set their prices 2 to 3 percent above the inflation rate. (Compare *Latin American Regional Reports,* RB-82-05, 28 May 1982; Mendonca de Barros and Graham, 1978:7-11.) Restrictions on interest articulation (aggregation) may have facilitated intentions to redistribute income from the poorer to the richer segments of Brazilian society. Finally, international lenders may have made more loans to Brazil because they believed the state's entrepreneurial-redistributive intermediation would produce the kind of growth that would ensure the prompt servicing of debts. But, in actuality, the manner in which the reform function of economic development was managed by Brazilian authorities could have had little or no effect on (aggregate) output; the pattern in figure 1 (Brazil) could be attributable more to movements *along* the state reform line than to any alterations in the "location" of goods market equilibria.

There is evidence to support just such a conclusion. To begin with, recent reviews of the literature on income inequality in Brazil have raised questions about the success (effects) of attempts to create a particular "consumption profile" in that country. In particular, they show that many of the existing studies of this topic — the results of which have been taken as fact by other researchers — are flawed in the way they treat unreported earnings, zero-income families, wage data, and other indicators of income inequality. For instance, Baloyra (1982) merely refers to the *number* of studies that have confirmed the effects of the government's policies. Alves (1982b) and Serra (1979) use data from studies shown to be seriously deficient; i.e., they use minimum wage data that is seriously affected by coverage of reporting firms (cf. Pfefferman and Webb, 1979:49-58; Taylor, et al., 1980:chp. 10, 302-06). The Pfefferman and Webb study is itself the object of criticism (*Latin American Regional Reports,* RB-80-04, 25 April 1980).

These reviews raise questions about our ability to ascertain the larger macro-level effects of, and the necessity of, government's redistributive policies. This is especially true if one considers the fact that, in most cases, inferences about trends in inequality have been made on the basis of two or three observations across ten or more years; and few analysts have assessed, systematically, the sensitivity of their results either to measurement problems or to contextual factors.

For example, Morley and Smith (1973) claim that, within reasonable limits, income redistribution has little, if any, impact on growth patterns. The authors assess the robustness of their conclusions against a number of alternative redistribution schemes. And they acknowledge various measurement problems. But, to be complete, they should more fully analyze the sensitivity of their results to alternative *parameterizations* of their model.

In the same spirit, contextual factors must be addressed. For instance, Serra (1979) has made a strong case for the claim that "the rapid growth (of Brazil) between 1968 and 1974 was not the result of some superior skill of the authoritarian regime at capitalist accumulation, but rather of a particular combination of favorable conditions of the domestic economy and of trade and capital conditions in the world market" (Serra, 1979:162).

Taylor and his associates (1980) have produced more nuanced and analytically rigorous studies of Brazilian income distribution. At a micro level, their work shows that the government's policies affected minimum wages which in turn affected median wages in the manufacturing sector, and, conceivably, such indicators of the quality of life as infant mortality. They also provide evidence that the negative effect of minimum wages on Brazilian employment levels would not necessarily have been severe. This same conclusion is reached in one of their more macro-level analysis — an analysis based on simulations of a large-scale, general equilibrium model of the Brazilian economy. The lesson drawn from these studies is that "under other socio-economic policies ranging from a more humane tax structure up through outright expropriation, growth could have been maintained or accelerated without making workers worse off" (Taylor, et al., 1980:327).

Recent reviews of the literature of Brazilian (re)distribution thus show that the conventional account of that country's indebted economic growth rests on weak, empirical footings. There is good reason to entertain unconventional explanations for the Brazilian pattern like that suggested by my diagrammatic analysis. This competing account holds that, in Brazil, the state reform and state entrepreneurship lines were both relatively flat, and the former equilibrium condition is essentially fixed, or d was effectively zero. The smooth increases in I and Y then come about more as a consequence of externally financed state entrepreneurship than as a result of any substantial alteration in autonomous demand attributable to income redistribution (figure 17). It follows that a transfer of income to the most disadvantaged groups in the population might have affected the willingness of lenders to finance the entrepreneurial activities of Brazilian governments but only because the international financial community (and ruling elites) *believed* that changes in the consumption profile would have a deleterious impact on economic growth. In actuality, a modest income redistribution would not, in itself, have had a major effect on aggregate demand; it would have had little effect on Brazil's ability to meet its financial obligations. [Of course, one might argue that the alteration of the consumption profile was intended to serve the short-term interests of the owners of particular industries, e.g., the foreign corporations who control the automobile industry. However, indications are that for many of the authorities, income redistribution was considered a means to promote growth in a variety of industries, many of which were owned by Brazilian natives (and, of course, by the state). Also, it seems likely that a large increase in output would be needed to significantly reduce demands for entrepreneurial assistance from the Brazilian state. And it is plausible that the impact of indebtedness on aggregate demand was large *relative to the propensity to spend current income* (but see Serra's discussion of the trends in capital goods importation in Collier, 1979:133). So, it may well be that the representation in figure 17 does capture the Brazilian experience.]

The fact that no effort was made to redress social inequality — indeed, the government repressed wage demands and cut social spending — has tremendous implications for the Brazilian government's ability to promote the continuation of indebted economic growth. Because authorities were willing and able to provide the political guarantees they and international lenders believed were necessary, Brazil was allowed to amass almost unlimited debt in the 1970s. For all practical purposes, policy makers were not preoccupied with the pursuit of any indebtedness target; rather, they sought to promote growth which, in turn, would legitimize the restrictions they had imposed on political freedoms (McDonough, 1980; Baloyra, 1982). As their profits grew, in some cases by an estimated 2600 percent (Alves, 1982b;795), lenders encouraged still further borrowing, based once more on the presumption that governments would effectively manage demands for income redistribution and, concomitantly, for political liberalization. In this way, the (shared) belief in the necessity for entrepreneurial-redistributive policies eventually created a situation in which the political and economic fortunes of Brazil posed a threat to the viability of the world's financial system. Needless to say, factors such as the rise in Eurobanking and its recycling problems, and Brazil's resource

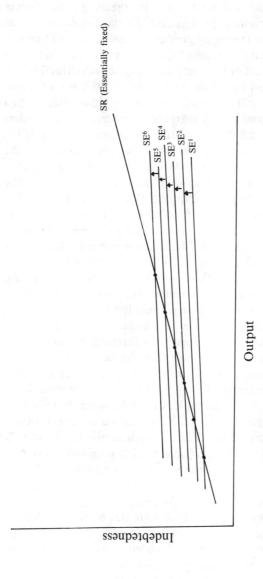

Figure 17. A Competing Explanation for the Brazilian Pattern of Indebted Economic Growth: The Consequences of Externally Financed State Entrepreneurship When Attempts to Promote Income Inequality Have Essentially No Impact on the Position of the SR Line

69

endowment and large market size also encouraged lending.

The negotiation of Brazil's debts has had far-reaching consequences for the politics of its economic development. By the end of the 1970s, international lenders were exercising greater caution in making loans to their Brazilian clients, and demanding higher interest and shorter terms as a hedge against the threat of slow debt servicing or even default (*Latin American Regional Report* RB-82-08, 17 September 1982; *World Financial Markets,* August 1982:7). Even with these restrictions, Brazil raised $3.6 billion in international capital markets in summer, 1982. Lenders also began to cooperate with the International Monetary Fund (IMF) in seeking a solution to the emerging debt crisis. But the exigencies of the "lender's trap" prevented lenders and IMF officials from imposing constraints on Brazil like those of 1964, when the IMF veto delimited the options available to the Goulart government (Wallerstein, 1980:25-34). This is not to suggest that the Figueiredo regime could or would have repudiated its debts. Unlike the Vargas administration, which defaulted on its foreign debts some decades earlier, that government relied heavily on international capital and technology; the fortunes of Brazil's economy were (are) intimately linked to global markets. The point is merely that, as a consequence of the history of indebted economic growth, Brazil's bargaining position was (is) much stronger than it was twenty years ago. As a consequence, Brazilian authorities have had a somewhat easier time extracting concessions from the international financial community. At the very least, their "eagerness" to meet their financial obligations has been muted by the realization that they have leverage over their creditors. [Of course, Brazilian authorities have not had an easy time negotiating concessions from the IMF. For example, Carlos Langoni, Brazil's Central Bank president, resigned over what he considered an unrealistic and unfair set of stabilization targets (*Latin American Weekly Report,* 20 September 1983). But the IMF also has agreed to overlook substantial discrepancies in Brazil's economic performance, discrepancies which can be traced, in part, to the workings of the liberalized political process in that country (*Wall Street Journal,* 7, November 1983).]

The strategy of the Brazilian economic team has been influenced by the political consequences of past efforts to renegotiate their country's debts, especially the outcome of former President Kubitschek's attempts to formulate an acceptable stabilization program in the early 1960s. However, the impact of the politics of Brazil's indebted economic growth extends far beyond the memory of this single encounter with IMF "orthodoxy." The manner in which Brazil's financial obligations have been renegotiated also is an outgrowth of political developments within that country — themselves consequences of the past policies of entrepreneurial-redistributive intermediation.

Over time, the very practices which contributed to Brazil's credit-worthiness has produced serious challenges to governmental authority. By the end of the 1960s, the regime found itself unable to control the bureaucracy that had been installed to repress demands for redistribution and liberalization. The state security apparatus became a threat to the well-being of Brazilian elites, and the government had more and more difficulty directing its activities. In addition, the regime faced growing opposition within the military to the reliance on international lenders and to the resurgence of direct foreign investment (Alves, 1982b; chp. 10; Baloyra, 1982). These problems, coupled with the oil crisis, led to the implementation of a "Master Plan" for "abertura," a *controlled* opening of the political system designed to reestablish governmental authority and legitimize Brazil's development strategy. At roughly the same time, the effects of the prolonged suppression of unions surfaced in a series of strikes, and severe cuts in social programs erupted in waves of urban violence. By allowing employees to dismiss workers and by making some concessions to certain groups (Alves, 1982b; chp. 10, sec. 4), the government avoided making any major political or economic reforms. However, there are indications that the "political consciousness" of citizens has been raised as a result of the workings of the new multiparty system and the modest gains made by unions. There is growing evidence that authorities are also having difficulty managing both the economy and the electoral system (Alves, 1982b; chp. 10:725-27).

Most analysts agree that it would be exceedingly difficult for Brazilian authorities to return to those policies so instrumental in ensuring their credit-worthiness in the late 1960s and early 1970s. One scenario is that the government will attempt to repress the demands of some especially threatening opposition groups while, at the same time, seeking to co-opt other elements of the opposition with the kind of reforms instituted in the pacotes of April 1977 and September 1978. This suggests that there will be more and more domestic political constraints on the country's economic team in renegotiating Brazil's debts. For example, it appears that the initial delays in rescheduling Brazil's debt were caused by policy makers' fears of driving business and other groups into the opposition (Baloyra, 1982). Of course, the terms of settlements with Brazil's creditors also will depend on events within both the local and global economies, particularly the success of attempts to control inflation and to maintain an acceptable trade balance. According to an economic research body linked to the Brazilian planning ministry (IPEA), if the economy were to grow at 5 percent per year and exports were to *rise* by 16.6 percent per year, there could be a drop in the debt servicing ratio to 41.5 percent by 1990. "However, if Brazil's exports grow by 11.2 percent (the predicted rates of growth in world trade and world inflation) or, worse still, by only 8 percent (the predicted rate of growth of world inflation), IPEA believes that the debt ratio would rise to 114 percent and 180 percent, respectively" (*Latin American Regional Report,* RB-82-05, 28 May 1982:2).

In sum, Baloyra (1982) is correct in pointing out that contrary to Figueirdo's pronouncements after his election to the presidency that "the game will go on but if the opposition goes beyond established limits, I will pick up the ball and put a stop to it," Figueirdo enter(ed) the game at a time when no one in Brazil, including himself, could control its outcome, much less pick up the ball and go home (Baloyra, 1982:43). The implication of the present investigation is that, as a consequence of the politics of indebted economic growth, a wider range of Brazilian interest groups have more to say about how the game is played as well as how their financial obligations shape its outcome. In fact, it is conceivable that Brazil's transition to a "strong democracy" may proceed further than expected because of the political effects of the sequence of entrepreneurial and redistributive policies adopted in the 1960s and early 1970s and the "lenders' trap" that it spawned.

5

CONCLUSION

The phenomenon of indebted economic growth has been shown to be, in part, an outgrowth of the role Third World states played in promoting economic development. The corresponding pattern of state intermediation — a series of entrepreneurial-redistributive policies — has been analyzed to determine what, if any, alternative strategies states might have pursued in the 1960s and 1970s. We have examined reasons why indebted economic growth is so prevalent in Latin America as a whole, and Brazil in particular. The policies of Brazilian governments have been analyzed and evaluated, and implications of a history of indebted economic growth for the resolution of a country's (ongoing) "debt crisis" have been assessed.

The major finding of this investigation is that states may be able to achieve their growth targets through policies of entrepreneurial assistance and substitution alone; income inequality need not be promoted (tolerated) if lenders are willing to finance state entrepreneurship. The importance of this condition should not be underestimated; evidence suggests that the (mistaken) belief in the necessity for income maldistribution and/or an authoritarian approach to managing the reform function of economic development has much to do with why the financial obligations of Third World countries grew faster than the rate of their output. Indebted economic growth appears to have resulted from unrealistic expectations of borrowing governments and international lenders, expectations based on the (mistaken) beliefs in the efficacy of entrepreneurial-redistributive intermediation. Many accounts of Third World economic development agree that promotion of greater income equality is compatible with economic growth. In fact, some scholars have gone so far as to explore alternative, administrative schemes for pursuing income redistribution from the rich to the poor (see Frank and Webb, 1977; Ahn, 1983; Alberts and Brundeis, 1979; Taylor, et al., 1980). However, few of these studies recognize the constraints which the beliefs of international lenders place on the ability of governments to implement such policies. [These constraints are further documented and analyzed empirically in Freeman (1983).]

Future research will investigate contrasts in the indebted economic growth of different countries and different regions for answers to the questions posed about the variations within Latin America. In particular, case studies of Mexico, Peru, Chile and Colombia should demonstrate that the contrasts in these countries' patterns of indebted economic growth can be attributed in large part to similarities (differences) in their sequences of entrepreneurial-redistributive policies.

Preliminary studies indicate that this theoretical expectation will be confirmed. The Mexican experience differs from Brazil's in two important respects: (1) the discovery of oil greatly enhanced Mexico's creditworthiness in the eyes of international lenders, and (2) the more inclusionary corporatist form of government appears to have encouraged the pursuit of more welfare-related objectives by state enterprises (Trebat, 1981). There is evidence that social inequality was promoted for the sake of economic growth (Hamilton, 1975), but it appears that Mexico's political system, with its six-year presidency (Baloyra, 1982:64-65; Leal, 1975) and nonmilitary, party bureaucracy may well have generated a somewhat different — albeit by no means equitable — sequence of redistributive policies. The two most important questions in regard to the Mexican experience are: Did the alternative mode of political organization in Mexico serve to (dis)encourage foreign borrowing beyond that which would have occurred had oil *not* been discovered? Did the performance of the reform function in Mexico have any meaningful impact on the pattern in figure 1 (Mexico), i.e., was there any basis for the belief that the maldistribution of income actually contributed to the rate of growth that country, achieved in the 1960s and 1970s?

It seems clear that Mexico's burgeoning debt has provided it with some leverage over its creditors. Another question to be explored, therefore, is whether the constraints imposed by Mexico's internal politics have allowed the new administration to fully exploit its bargaining position in the debt negotiations. Former president José Lopez Portillo stated that "if the international context is not organized so [Mexico] can handle it, the deterioration of the countries of the South will drag down those of the North" (*The New York Times,* 1 October 1982:A2). Future research will attempt to determine the extent to which the new Mexican administration's apparent success in resolving its financial problems derives from an effective use of similar negotiating tactics.

The experiences of Peru, Chile and Colombia are different from those of Brazil and Mexico; the international financial community has had greater influence promoting the entrepreneurial-redistributive policies of the respective governments. In Peru, after 1968, the character of entrepreneurial assistance changed from support to "control." The Peruvian public sector expanded rapidly, often at the expense of foreign firms, including foreign banks (Fitzgerald, 1976). This expansion was only partly financed by external borrowing; initially, the state simply granted credit to itself for this purpose. When the Peruvian governments eventually encountered difficulties and sought more foreign funds for state enterprise, budget deficits and the financing of its trade imbalance, the international financial community imposed restrictions on the type and scope of entrepreneurial assistance the Peruvian regime could provide. [Riner (1982) argues that to some extent these difficulties were the outgrowth of lenders being unwilling and unable to coordinate their policies toward extending loans to the government. (See also Lipson, 1981.) In particular, Peruvian authorities were compelled to reopen certain investment opportunities to foreign investors, to reprivatize some state firms and to limit capital goods purchases by existing public enterprises (Stallings, 1979). Assumption (A) therefore may not hold for the entire period, 1967-1980; the government's willingness to assist the entrepreneurial function may not always have led to an upward adjustment in indebtedness. At some point, the excess assistance offered by the state led to external restrictions being placed on Peruvian policy makers. Note also that the stabilization policy imposed by commercial banks and the IMF had much to do with the slowdown in growth after 1976; cf. figure 1 (Peru).]

The Peruvian state continues to be actively engaged in the entrepreneurial function of growth. Indeed, its 1981-1985 development plan provides for $8.5 billion in public investment, almost 60 percent of which is to be financed externally. And, in keeping with the argument made here, the regime's ability to secure these funds apparently still depends on its willingness to sanction social inequality; "bankers say assumptions in (Peru's planned) economic model are feasible if the government can resist social and political pressures and push ahead with measures to reduce fiscal deficits and restrain inflation" (*Business Latin America,* 3 June 1981:174).

In sum, the qualitative similarity in the Peruvian and Brazilian patterns appears to derive in part from a (temporary) reliance on the same sequence of entrepreneurial-redistributive intermediation. But that similarity also masks some important differences with respect to the manner in which Peruvian authorities have been able to offer entre-preneurial assistance to national enterprise, namely, the effects of the imposition of external constraints on the level of indebtedness Peru is allowed to incur as well as the reality of direct intervention (by the IMF) in Peruvian policy making. Peruvian authorities, unlike their Mexican counterparts, thus do not "enjoy" a great deal of leverage over their creditors.

For a number of reasons, the Chilean case is the most difficult to interpret. To begin with, there is a question as to whether the pattern in figure 1 (Chile) accurately depicts the recent history of indebtedness and output in Chile. According to the World Bank's supplements, ex-ternal private *nonguaranteed* debt (outstanding and disbursed) ranged from 20 percent to 25 percent of external public debt for the years 1976-1978. However, according to the Chilean Central Bank, non-guaranteed external debt ranged from 42 percent to 73 percent of external public debt in this period (Bank Central de Chile, *Boletin Mensual* No. 628, Junio 1980). In other words, the Chilean Central Bank data suggest that, overall, the magnitude of Chile's debt was (is) much greater than that indicated by the World Bank's public debt figures and therefore the pattern of indebted economic growth might be somewhat different than that depicted in figure 1 (Chile).

In regard to the fidelity of the diagrammatic analysis, Chilean authorities renounced the practice of entrepreneurial substitution immediately after the fall of Allende in 1973 (Remmer, 1978:446). It is unclear, however, whether the relative importance of state enterprise, e.g., in terms of public investment, declinded precipitously. The government committed itself to greater reliance on private enterprise for the promo-tion of growth and for the provision of social services. So, it might appear that the pattern in figure 1 (Chile) cannot be attributed to the sequence of entrepreneurial-redistribution depicted in figure 12. However, recent studies indicate that lenders have forced the Chilean government to borrow heavily through their state enterprises, obstensibly "to prepare the market" for private borrowers. In this respect, the state holding company, Corporación de Femento de la Producción (CORFO), has continued to play an important role in promoting externally financed, native entrepreneurship. Riner (1982) reports that the extent of the Chilean Central Bank's role in arranging borrowing by one of its undertakings depends on "the experience and bargaining power of the public enter-prise" (Riner, 1982, n. 27). Finally, note that Allende's extensive program of social reform could conceivably have moved *both* the SR and SE lines to the northwest prior to 1973 [again compare figures 1 (Chile) and 12]. [Arrelano (1983) reports that between 1970 and 1972 the share of social expenditure to GDP increased from 19.9 to 25.2, while between 1972 and 1979 this ratio fell to 15.4. Evidence of American bankers' beliefs in the efficacy of the Chilean government development strategy can be found in such sources as the *International Herald Tribune* (22 September 1983). See Freeman (1983) for a discussion of recent developments in the negotiation of Chile's foreign debts, including the provision for state takeover of failing bank groups.]

Like Peru, the distinguishing feature of the Chilean experience has been the extent to which the international financial community has been willing and able to intervene either by imposing limits on the indebtedness Chile is allowed to incur or by influencing the content of the government's economic and social policies. The results depicted in figure 15 thus may help us understand the patterns of indebted economic growth in these two countries.

While entrepreneurial substitution is less prevalent in Colombia (but see Fernandez and O'Campo, 1975), the respective governments have been active in providing infrastructural facilities and loan guarantees for native enterprises. Authorities also have sought to promote social inequality and in that way violated the spirit of the Alliance for Progress (Speck, 1981). For the period 1979-1983 Colombia was expected to borrow an average of $1.35 billion per year, about 60 percent to be supplied by the World Bank and the International Development Bank. Most of these financial resources were to be invested in infrastructure and basic industries (74%) with only a small portion being devoted to the amelioration of social inequality and other human needs (9.7%). So it seems that in Colombia the policy sequence has embodied increasing entrepreneurial support with sanctions (promotion) of income inequality. Thus, it may be that here too the state entrepreneurship line shifted to the northwest along the (fixed) state reform line (figure 17).

Future research will also scrutinize the assumptions on which the diagrammatic analysis is based, and modify that framework in ways that render it more realistic and analytically powerful. For example, the reference to the importance of incorporating Mexico's oil revenue raises the issue of whether it is reasonable to assume that the goods market clears, or more generally, whether it is reasonable to focus exclusively on internal demand for goods and services. That is, whether it is reasonable to assume that in Third World countries an excess (internal) demand for goods and services leads to a compensatory increase in production and vice versa; this is assumption (A). A more realistic formulation would incorporate the impacts of fluctuations in export demand on local market equilibria and in that way allow an assessment of the effects of the global recession of the 1970s on patterns of indebted economic growth. Similarly, the assumption that indebtedness varies with the state's willingness to meet demands for entrepreneurial assistance and substitution limits the usefulness of the analysis, especially for the recent period when lenders and borrowers have been confronted with a debt "crisis." Relaxation of assumption (B) requires the construction of models for the (global) credit market and perhaps also explicit incorporation of the savings-investment balance. The work of the structuralists school of development economics and its offshoots would appear to offer the most useful guidelines as to how to proceed in this regard (Taylor, 1981, 1984).

APPENDIX

From equation (2), we know that under policy SE' the demand for entrepreneurial assistance is satisfied according to the relation:

$$\text{SE:} \qquad I = (\tfrac{1}{k})(SE' - \overline{DE} + |n|Y). \qquad (2)$$

It follows that the slope of the SE line is $(\tfrac{dI}{dY})_{SE} = \tfrac{|n|}{k}$. Also, from equation (5), we have, under the policy EQ', the equilibrium relation for the SR line:

$$\text{SR:} \qquad Y = (\tfrac{1}{1-b})(\overline{DG} + iI + dEQ'), \qquad (5)$$

which may be rewritten

$$I = (\tfrac{1}{i})[(1-b)Y - \overline{DG} + |d|EQ']. \qquad (5.1)$$

Hence we know that the slope of the SR line is $(\tfrac{dI}{dY})_{SR} = \tfrac{1-b}{i}$. Thus, we have

CASE I. The slope of the SR line exceeds the slope of the SE line if

$$\tfrac{1-b}{i} > \tfrac{|n|}{k} \text{ or } k(1-b) > i|n|;$$

CASE II. The slope of the SE line exceeds the slope of the SR line if

$$\tfrac{|n|}{k} > \tfrac{1-b}{i} \text{ or } i|n| > (1-b)k,$$

while if the slope of the two lines are equal, the relations are

CASE III. $k(1-b) = i|n|$ but $(\tfrac{1}{k})(SE' - \overline{DE}) \neq (\tfrac{1}{i})(-\overline{DG} + |d|EQ')$;

CASE IV. $k(1-b) = i|n|$ and $(\tfrac{1}{k})(SE' - \overline{DE}) = (\tfrac{1}{i})(-\overline{DG} + |d|EQ')$.

To discover the identity of the (I, Y) pair which is the joint policy equilibria — the combination of indebtedness and output which both clears the goods market and satisfies demands for entrepreneurial assistance — we substitute the formula for I in equation (2) into equation (5) and obtain

$$Y = (\tfrac{1}{1-b})[\overline{DG} + i(\tfrac{1}{k})(SE' - \overline{DE} + |n|Y) + dEQ'],$$

from which it follows that

$$Y^* = [\frac{k}{k(1-b)-i|n|}][\overline{DG} + \frac{i}{k}(SE' - \overline{DE}) + dEQ'].$$

In the same way, we can, by substituting the formula for Y in equation (5) into equation (2), find the equilibrium level of indebtedness:

$$I^* = [\frac{(1-b)}{k(1-b)-i|n|}][SE' - \overline{DE} + \frac{|n|}{(1-b)}(\overline{DG} + dEQ')].$$

REFERENCES

Abbott, G. C. 1981. International Indebtedness of Less Developed Countries: Structure, Growth, Indicators. *Aussenwirtschraft,* 36 Jahrgang, Heft IV, Zurich: Schulthess: S.340-51.

Ahn, Young Sop. 1983. Authoritarian Equality: Korea in Comparative Perspective. Unpublished paper. Cambridge: MIT Department of Political Science.

Alberts, T. and C. Brundeis. 1978. *Growth Versus Equity: The Brazilian Case in Light of the Peruvian and the Cuban Experiences.* Monograph. University of Lund Research Policy Institute.

Alves, Maria Helena Moreira. 1982a. Limitations on the Rights of Citizens: The National Security State in Brazil (1964-198?). Paper presented at the XII World Congress of the International Political Science Assn., Rio de Janeiro, August 9-14.

_____. 1982b. The Formation of the National Security State: The State and the Opposition in Military Brazil. Unpublished Ph.D. dissertation. Cambridge: MIT.

Ames, B. 1979. Survival Strategies and Expenditure Tradeoffs in Latin America. Political Science Paper No. 42. St. Louis: Washington University.

Aronson, J. 1977. *Money and Power: Banks and the World Monetary System.* Beverly Hills: Sage.

Arrelano, J.P. 1983. The Impact on Social Policies of the Military Regimes Economic Model. Paper presented at conference on Chile, ten years after the Coup. Harvard University, October 21-22.

Asher, W. 1982. The International Export and New Development Strategies. Paper presented at the Conference on International Stability and Cooperation, Minneapolis, October 12-14.

Bacha, E. L. 1976. *Os mitos de uma decada: Eusaios de economica brasileira.* Rio de Janeiro: Paz e Terra.

Bacha, E. L. and L. Taylor. 1980. Brazilian Income Distribution in the 1960s: "Facts," Model Results, and the Controversy. In *Models of Growth and Distribution for Brazil,* Taylor, et al., eds. pp. 296-342. New York: Oxford University Press.

Bacha, E. L. and C. Diaz-Alejandro. 1982. *International Financial Intermediation: A Long and Tropical View.* Princeton: Princeton Essays in International Finance, No. 147.

Baer, W. 1973. The Brazilian Boom 1968-1972: An Explanation and Interpretation. *World Development* 1(18):1-15.

Bear, W., I. Kerstenetsky and A. Villela. 1973. The Changing Role of the State in the Brazilian Economy. *World Development* 1(11):23-24.

_____.1974. The Role of Government Enterprises in Latin America's Industrialization. In *Fiscal Policy for Industrialization and Development in Latin America,* D. Geithman, ed. pp. 263-81. Gainesville: University of

Florida Press.

Baer, W., R. Newfarmer, and T. Trebat. 1977. On State Capitalism in Brazil: Some New Issues and Questions. *Inter-American Economic Affairs 30(3):69-91.*

Baer, W. and A. V. Villela. 1980. The Changing Nature of Development Banking in Brazil. *Journal of Interamerican Studies and World Affairs* 22(4):423-40.

Baer, W. and A. Figueroa. 1981. State Enterprise and the Distribution of Income: Brazil and Peru. In *Authoritarian Capitalism: Brazil's Contemporary Economic and Political Development,* T.C. Bruneau and P. Faucher, eds. pp. 59-84. Boulder: Westview.

Balassa, B., ed. 1977. *Economic Progress, Private Values and Public Policy: Essays in Honor of William Fellner.* New York: North Holland.

Baloyra, E.A. 1982. The Deterioration of Authoritarian Regimes: Is Brazil Undergoing a Process of Democratic Transition? Paper presented at the XII World Congress of the International Political Science Assn., Rio de Janeiro, August 9-14.

Bennett, D. and K. Sharpe. 1980. The State as Banker and Entrepreneur. *Comparative Politics* January: 165-89.

_____. 1982. The State and Dependent Development in Mexico, 1917-1970. Paper presented at the Annual Meeting of the American Political Science Assn., Denver, Colorado, September 2-5.

Bluestone, B. and B. Harrison. 1982. *The Deindustrialization of America: Plant Closings Community Abandonment and the Dismantling of Basic Industry.* New York: Basic Books.

Brau, E. and R. C. Williams, et al. 1983. Recent Multilateral Debt Restructurings with Official and Bank Creditors. Occasional Paper No. 25. Washington, D. C.: IMF.

Bruneau, T. C. and P. Faucher. 1981. *Authoritarian Capitalism: Brazil's Contemporary Economic and Political Development.* Boulder: Westview.

Cameron, D. R. 1978. The Expansion of the Public Economy: A Comparative Analysis. *American Political Science Review* 74(4):1243-61.

Cameron, R., ed. 1972. *Banking and Economic Development: Some Lessons of History.* New York: Oxford University Press.

Caporaso, J. 1980. Dependence Theory: Continuities and Discontinuities in Development Studies. *International Organization* 34(4):605-28.

Cardoso, F. 1979. On the Characterization of Authoritarian Regimes in Latin America. In *The New Authoritarianism in Latin America,* D. Collier, ed. pp. 35-57. Princeton: Princeton University Press.

Cardoso, F. and E. Faletto. 1979. *Dependency and Development in Latin America,* translated by M. Urguidi. Berkeley: University of California Press.

Choksi, A. 1979. State Intervention in the Industrialization of Developing Countries: Selected Issues. *Staff Working Paper* No. 341. Washington, D.C.:

World Bank.

Churchill, Anthony. 1974. Comment/Discussion. In *Fiscal Policy for Industrialization and Development in Latin America,* D. Geithman, ed. p. 290. Gainesville: University of Florida Press.

Collier, D., ed. 1979. *The New Authoritarianism in Latin America.* Princeton: Princeton University Press.

Collier, D. and R. Collier. 1979. Inducements versus Constraints: Disaggregating "Corporatism." *American Political Science Review* 73(4):967-86.

Cornelius, W. A. 1975. *The Politics of the Migrant Poor in Mexico City.* Stanford: Stanford University Press.

Delfim Netto, Antonio. 1973. Foreword. In *Distribúticão da renda e desenvolvimento econômico do Brasil,* Carlos Geraldo Langoni. Rio de Janeiro: Editora Expresaõ e Cultura.

Dornbusch, R. and S. Fischer. 1978. *Macroeconomics.* New York: McGraw-Hill.

Duvall, R. and J. Freeman. 1983. The Techno-Bureaucratic Elite and the Entrepreneurial State in Dependent Industrialization. *American Political Science Review* 77(3):569-87.

Economic Commission for Latin America (ECLA). 1964. Fifteen Years of Economic Policy in Brazil. *Economic Bulletin for Latin America* 9:153-214.

_____.1974. Public Enterprises: Their Present Significance and Their Potential in Development. *Economic Bulletin for Latin America* 19:1-70.

Evans, P. 1976. Continuities and Contradictions in the Evolution of Brazilian Dependence. *Latin American Perspectives* 3(2):30-54.

_____. 1979. *Dependent Development: The Alliance of Multinational, State and Local Capital in Brazil.* Princeton: Princeton University Press.

Fagen, R., ed. 1979. *Capitalism and the State in U.S.-Latin American Relations.* Stanford: Stanford University Press.

Feder, G. 1982. Growth and External Borrowing in Trade Gap Economies of Less Developed Countries. *Aussenwirtschraft* 36, Jahrang, Heft IV. Zurich: Schulthess, S.:381-95.

Fernandez, R. and J. O'Campo. 1975. The Andean Pact and State Capitalism in Colombia. *Latin American Perspectives* 2(3):19-35.

Fitzgerald, E.V.K. 1976. The State and Economic Development: Peru Since 1968. *Occasional Paper* Number 42. New York: Cambridge University Press.

Frank, C.R. and R. Webb. 1977. *Income Distribution and Growth in Less Developed Countries.* Washington, D.C.:Brookings.

Frank, I. 1980. *Foreign Enterprise in Developing Countries.* New York: C.E.D.

Freeman, J. 1982a. State Entrepreneurship and Dependent Development. *American Journal of Political Science* 26(1):90-112.

_____. 1982b. International Economic Relations and the Politics of

Mixed Economies. Paper presented at the XII World Congress of the International Political Science Assn., Rio de Janeiro, August 9-14.

_____. 1983. The Politics of the Third World Debt Crisis. Unpublished. Cambridge: MIT Department of Political Science.

_____. 1985. *The Politics of Mixed Economies.* Forthcoming.

Freeman, J. and R. Duvall. 1984. International Economic Relations and the Entrepreneurial State. *Economic Development and Cultural Change* 32(4):373-400.

Freeman, J. and D. Snidal. 1982. Diffusion, Development and Democratization: Enfranchisement in Western Europe. *Canadian Journal of Political Science* 15(2):299-329.

Frieden, J. 1981. Third World Industrialization: International Finance and State Capitalism in Mexico, Brazil, Algeria and South Korea. *International Organization* 35(3):407-31.

Gantt, A. and G. Dutto. 1968. Financial Performance of Government-Owned Corporations in Less Developed Countries. *IMF Staff Papers* 25:102-42.

Geithman, D., ed. 1974. *Fiscal Policy for Industrialization and Development in Latin America.* Gainesville: University of Florida Press.

Gillis, M. 1980. The Role of State Enterprises in Economic Development. *Social Research* 47(2):248-89.

Girvan, N. 1980. Swallowing the IMF Medicine in the 1970s. *Development Dialogue* 2:55-74.

Hamilton, N. 1975. Mexico: The Limits of State Autonomy. *Latin American Perspectives* 2(2):81-108.

Hirschman, A. 1958. *The Strategy of Economic Development.* New Haven: Yale University Press.

_____. 1971. *A Bias for Hope.* New Haven: Yale University Press.

_____. 1973. The Changing Tolerance for Income Inequality in the Course of Economic Development. *Quarterly Journal of Economics* 87(4):543-66.

_____. 1979. The Turn to Authoritarianism in Latin America and the Search for Its Economic Determinants. In *The New Authoritarianism in Latin America,* D. Collier, ed. pp. 61-98. Princeton: Princeton University Press.

Jones, L. 1975. *Public Enterprise and Economic Development: The Korean Case.* Seoul: Korean Development Institute.

_____. 1981. Public Enterprise for Whom? Perverse Distributional Consequences of Public Operational Decisions. Paper presented at the International Symposium on the Economic Performance of Public Enterprise. Islamabad, Pakistan, November 24-28.

Katz, C. J., V. A. Mahler, and M. G. Franz. 1983. The Impact of Taxes on Growth and Distribution in Developed Capitalist Countries. *American Political Science Review* 77(4): 871-86.

Kindleberger, C. P. 1981. Debt Situation of the Developing Countries in Historical Perspective (1800-1945). *Aussenwirtschraft* 36, Jahrang, Heft IV. Zurich: Schulthess, S. 372-80.

Kuznets, S. 1979. *Growth, Population and Income Distribution.* New York: W.W. Norton.

Leal, J. F. 1975. The Mexican State: 1915-1973, A Historical Interpretation. *Latin American Perspectives* 2(2):48-63.

Lipson, C. 1981. The International Organization of Third World Debt. *International Organization* 34(4):603-31.

Malloy, J.M. 1977. Authoritarianism and Corporation in Latin America: The Modal Pattern. In *Authoritarianism and Corporation in Latin America,* J. M. Malloy, ed. pp. 3-22. Pittsburgh: University of Pittsburgh Press.

Marsh, R. M. 1979. Does Democracy Hinder Economic Development in the Latecomer Developing Nations? *Comparative Social Research* 2:215-48.

Marshall, T. H. 1950. *Citizenship and Social Class.* Cambridge: University Press.

Martins, Luciano. 1981. Estatizacao' da Economia "Privatizacao" do Estado? In *Authoritarian Capitalism: Brazil's Contemporary Economic and Political Development,* T. C. Bruneau and P. Faucher, eds. pp. 79-80. Boulder: Westview.

McDonough, P. 1980. Developmental Priorities Among Brazilian Elite. *Economic Development and Cultural Change* 29(2):535-59.

—————————. 1981. *Power and Ideology in Brazil.* Princeton: Princeton University Press.

McKnight, L. 1983. Brazilian Debt and (Inter)Dependency: A Historical Review. Unpublished paper. Cambridge: MIT Department of Political Science.

Mendonca de Barros, J.R. and D. H. Graham. 1978. The Brazilian Economic Miracle Revisited: Private and Public Sector Initiative in a Market Economy. *Latin American Research Review* 13(3):5-38.

Molinari, B. C. 1977. The State and the Bourgeoisie in the Peruvian Fishmeal Industry. *Latin American Perspectives* 3:103-21.

Morley, S. A. and G. W. Smith. 1973. The Effect of Changes in the Distribution of Income on Labor, Foreign Investment, and Growth in Brazil. In *Authoritarian Brazil: Origins, Policies and Future,* A. Stepan, ed. pp. 119-41. New Haven: Yale University Press.

Newfarmer, R. S. and W. F. Meuller. 1975. *Multinational Corporations in Brazil and Mexico: Structural Sources of Economic and Non-Economic Power.* Washington, D. C.: GPO.

O'Connor, J. 1973. *The Fiscal Crisis of the State.* New York: St. Martin's Press.

Offe, C. 1982. Competitive Party Democracy and the Keynesian Welfare State: Factors of Stability and Disorganization. Paper presented at the XII World

Congress of the International Political Science Assn., Rio de Janeiro, August 9-14.

Okun, A. 1975. *Equity and Efficiency: The Big Tradeoff.* Washington, D.C.: Brookings.

Perez, A. 1980. Investment and Financing Aspects of State Petroleum Enterprises. In *State Petroleum Enterprises in Developing Countries,* United Nations Centre for Natural Resources, Energy and Transport. pp. 141-50. New York: Pergamon.

Petras, J. 1977. State Capitalism and the Third World. *Development and Change* 8:1-17.

Pfefferman, G. P. and R. Webb. 1979. The Distribution of Income in Brazil. *Working Paper* No. 356. Washington, D.C.:World Bank.

Przeworski, A. and F. Cortes. 1971. Sistemas partidistas, movilzacion electoral y electoral, y la establidad de sociedadas capitalistas. *Revista Latinoamericana de Ciencia Politica* 2(2):220-41.

Przeworski, A. and M. Wallerstein. 1982. Democratic Capitalism at the Crossroads. *Democracy* (July):52-68.

Quijano, A. 1971. *Nationalism and Capitalism in Peru: A Study in Neo-Imperialism.* New York: Monthly Review Press.

Remmer, K. L. 1979. Public Policy and Regime Consolidation: The First Five Years of the Chilean Junta. *Journal of Developing Areas* 13 (July):441-61.

Riner, D. L. 1982. Private Banks and the Politics of Economic Policy Making in Peru and Chile. Paper presented at the 1982 Meeting of the American Political Science Assn., Denver, Colorado, September 2-5.

Schmitter, P. 1971. Military Intervention, Political Competitiveness and Public Policy in Latin America. In *On Military Intervention,* M. Janowitz and J. van Doorn, eds. pp. 425-506. Rotterdam:Rotterdam University Press.

Serra, José. 1979. Three Mistaken Theses Regarding the Connection Between Industrialization. In *The New Authoritarianism in Latin America,* D. Collier, ed. pp. 99-164. Princeton: Princeton University Press.

Sheahan, J. 1980. Market-Oriented Economic Policies and Political Repression in Latin America. *Economic Development and Cultural Change* 3(2):267-91.

Simonsen, M. H. 1974a. Preface. In *O Modelo Brasileiro,* M. Millo Filho. p. 2. Rio de Janeiro: Bloch.

——————. 1974b. *Brazil 2002.* Rio de Janeiro.

——————. 1977. The Rise of Brazil. *Commentary* 63(1):49-50.

Speck, M. 1981. Colombia: Growth Without Equity. *International Policy Report* February.

Stallings, B. 1979. Peru and U.S. Banks: Privatization of Financial Relations. In *Capitalism and the State in U.S.-Latin American Relations,* R. Fagen, ed. pp. 217-53. Stanford: Stanford University Press.

Stepan, A. 1973. *Authoritarian Brazil: Origins, Policies and Future.* New

Haven: Yale University Press.

_____. 1978. *The State and Society: Peru in Comparative Perspective*. Princeton: Princeton University Press.

Taylor, L. 1979. *Macro Models for Developing Countries*. New York: McGraw-Hill.

_____. 1981. North-South Trade and Southern Growth: Bleak Prospects from a Structuralist Point of View. *Journal of International Economics* 11:589-602.

_____. 1984. A North-South Debt Crisis. Unpublished. Cambridge: MIT Department of Economics.

Taylor, L., et al., eds. 1980. *Models of Growth and Distribution for Brazil*. New York:Oxford University Press.

Trebat, T. J. 1981. Public Enterprises in Brazil and Mexico: A Comparison of Origins and Performance. In *Authoritarian Capitalism: Brazil's Contemporary Economic and Political Development,* T. C. Bruneau and P. Faucher, eds. pp. 41-58. Boulder: Westview.

_____. 1983. *Brazil's State-Owned Enterprises: A Case Study of the State as Entrepreneur*. New York: Cambridge University Press.

Tyler, William G. 1974. Comment/Discussion. In *Fiscal Policy for Industrialization and Development in Latin America,* D. Geithman, ed. pp. 286-90. Gainesville: University of Florida Press.

United Nations Centre for Natural Resources, Energy and Transport. 1980. *State Petroleum Enterprises in Developing Countries*. New York: Pergamon Press.

Wallerstein, M. 1980. The Collapse of Democracy in Brazil: Its Economic Determinants. *Latin American Research Review* 15(3):3-43.

_____. 1982. The Welfare Economics of Capital Accumulation: A Literature Review. Paper delivered at the Annual Meeting of the American Political Science Association, Denver, Colorado, September 2-5.

Weede, E. and H. Tiefenbach. 1981. Some Recent Explanations of Income Inequality. *International Studies Quarterly* 25(2):255-82.

Whiting, V.R. 1981. Transnational Enterprise and the State in Mexico. Unpublished Ph.D. dissertation, Cambridge: Department of Government, Harvard University.

_____. 1982. State Intervention in Brazil and Mexico: Theoretical Considerations for a Comparative Study. Paper delivered at the XII World Congress of the International Political Science Association, Rio de Janeiro, August 9-14.

THE ANNALS

of The American Academy *of*
Political *and* Social Science

RICHARD D. LAMBERT, *Editor*
ALAN W. HESTON, *Associate Editor*

CHINA IN TRANSITION

Special Editor: Marvin E. Wolfgang

As China and the United States move together through the 1980s and 1990s, the legal, economic, and ethical issues facing China are also significant to the United States. Population and migration control . . . criminal justice and civil rights . . . investment of capital in hotels, in high technology, and in nuclear power . . . all are topics of major concern.

This issue, prepared for the 87th annual meeting of the American Academy of Political and Social Science, furthers our understanding of the problems and potentials of China. Academic and political science experts examine legal education, internal politics, population control, urbanization, rural agriculture, and modernization. They also explore the relationships among China, the USSR, and the United States. Original and intriguing, these papers constitute a timely portrait of a country in the midst of dramatic change.

Volume 476   November 1984

Enter your Academy membership today!

A subscription to **The Annals** is available to individuals only through membership in The American Academy of Political and Social Science, one of the world's oldest and most distinguished professional associations. Each bimonthly volume of **The Annals** presents current, insightful articles on a single emerging social issue, all invited by an expert guest editor. Each volume also contains **The Annals'** timely Book Department—a knowledgeable review of new literature in the social sciences.

Your one-year Academy membership includes six bimonthly volumes of **The Annals.**

One-year Academy membership:
$26 — **The Annals** paper edition
$39 — **The Annals** cloth edition

One-year institutional subscription:
$45 — **The Annals** paper edition
$60 — **The Annals** cloth edition

Please send orders to **The Annals,** in care of

SAGE PUBLICATIONS
The Publishers of Professional Social Science
275 South Beverly Drive, Beverly Hills, California 90212

CAIRO PAPERS IN SOCIAL SCIENCE
بحوث القاهرة فى العلوم الإجتماعية

The CAIRO PAPERS IN SOCIAL SCIENCE provides a medium for the dissemination of research in social, economic and political development conducted by visiting and local scholars working in Egypt and the Middle East. Produced at the American University in Cairo since 1977, CAIRO PAPERS has published more than 20 issues of collected articles and monographs on a variety of topics. Beginning January 1983, issues will appear on a quarterly basis. . Future topics include:

> THE POLITICAL ECONOMY OF REVOLUTIONARY IRAN
> URBAN RESEARCH STRATEGIES FOR EGYPT
> THE HISTORY AND ROLE OF THE EGYPTIAN PRESS
> SOCIAL SECURITY AND THE FAMILY IN EGYPT
> THE NATIONALIZATION OF ARABIC AND ISLAMIC
>   EDUCATION IN EGYPT: DAR AL-ULUM AND AL-AZHAR
> NON-ALIGNMENT IN A CHANGING WORLD

In addition, we plan to publish a special index of survey research conducted by Egyptian research centers and agencies which will be offered at a discount rate to our subscribers.

****
NAME: INSTITUTION:

ADDRESS:

CITY: STATE OR COUNTRY:

VOLUME SIX ORDERS
     INDIVIDUAL (US $15 or L.E.8)   INSTITUTIONAL (US $25 or L.E.10)
                                           Please indicate if standing order:
BACK ORDERS
     SINGLE ISSUES (US $4 or L.E.3)   _____VOLUME 4 (US $15 or L.E.8)
Please indicate title and author:

Enclosed is a check or money order for_____payable to THE AMERICAN UNIVERSITY IN CAIRO (CAIRO PAPERS).

Signature or authorization:

****
Inquiries or orders originating in the   Those originating elsewhere should
USA should be sent to: be sent to:

    CAIRO PAPERS IN SOCIAL SCIENCE   CAIRO PAPERS IN SOCIAL SCIENCE
    American University in Cairo   American University in Cairo
    866 U.N. Plaza   P.O. Box 2511
    New York, N.Y. 10017   Cairo, Egypt

If you are interested in the study of politics
and government, you are invited to join

THE SOUTHERN POLITICAL SCIENCE ASSOCIATION

MEMBERSHIP INCLUDES

THE JOURNAL OF POLITICS

THE JOURNAL OF POLITICS is a quarterly devoted to enriching and advancing the knowledge of politics. Inside its pages all methods, positions, conceptualizations, and techniques are expounded by authors who know their subjects and who back their ideas with careful research and positive scholarship. There is no bias in THE JOURNAL OF POLITICS—toward theory, American politics, or anything else. It is an open journal. Missing it is missing an adventure into the character of political variety.

Upon receipt of this form you will begin a one-year membership in The Southern Political Science Association, including a subscription to THE JOURNAL OF POLITICS.

_____ Individual .... $ 17.00
_____ Student or Retired .... $ 10.00
_____ Institution .... $ 25.00
_____ Foreign Postage (additional) .... $ 5.50

Name_____

Address _____

_____

_____
                                                      Zip Code

Please make check or money order payable to THE JOURNAL OF POLITICS. Send to:

THE JOURNAL OF POLITICS
University of Florida
Gainesville, FL, USA 32611

Established 1928

Isn't it time to subscribe?

Pacific
Affairs

Vol. 57, No. 4   Winter 1984-85

An International Review of Asia and the Pacific

Pacific Affairs
University of British Columbia
Vancouver, BC, Canada V6T 1W5

Published Quarterly

Subscription rates: for individuals, $25 per year; for institutions, $30 per year.
Add $5 for postage outside North America.

Journal *of* Peace Research

Vol. 22 No. 1 1985

Focus On: *Petter Wallensteen:* Détente – What Went Wrong?
Stein Tønnesson: The Longest Wars: Indochina 1945-1975
J. Samuel Fitch: The Garrison State in America: A Content Analysis of Trends in the Expectations of Violence
James H. Lebovic: Capabilities in Context: National Attributes and Foreign Policy in the Middle East
Georg Sørensen: Peace and Development: Looking for the Right Track
Review Essay: *Lars Mjøset:* The Limits of Neoclassical Institutionalism
Book Notes
Books Received

COOPERATION AND CONFLICT
NORDIC JOURNAL OF INTERNATIONAL POLITICS

Published quarterly for the Nordic Cooperation Committe for International Politics, including Conflict and Peace Research, by Universitetsforlaget, Journals Dept., Oslo, Norway. It is the only journal in the English language devoted to studies of the foreign policies of the Nordic countries and to studies of international politics by Nordic scholars.

The subscription price per volume (1985 rates), payable in advance, is: Institutions: USD 30.00 (NOK 180,-), Individuals: USD 24.00 (NOK 144,-), Students: USD 15.00 (NOK 93,-).

Editor: Lauri Karvonen, Department of Political Science, Åbo Academy, 20500 Åbo 50, Finland.

Orders can be placed with Universitetsforlaget, Subscription Division, P.O. Box 2959 Tøyen, 0608 Oslo 6, Norway, and US Office: P.O. Box 258, Irvington-on-Hudson, NY 10533, USA.

Contents Vol. XX, No. 1, March 1985:

COOPERATION AND CONFLICT   ORDER FORM

I wish to become a subscriber from No. 1, 1985

☐ Institutions USD 30.00 (NOK 180,-)   ☐ cheque enclosed
☐ Individuals USD 24.00 (NOK 144,-)   ☐ please send invoice
☐ Students USD 15.00 (NOK 93,-)

Name: ....

Address: ....

Issues will be sent to you as soon as payment is received.
UNIVERSITETSFORLAGET A/S, P.O. Box 2959 Tøyen, 0608 Oslo 6, Norway

UNIVERSITETSFORLAGET

119a